DEEP LEARNING CRASH COURSE
FOR BEGINNERS
WITH PYTHON

THEORY AND APPLICATIONS OF ARTIFICIAL NEURAL
NETWORKS, CNN, RNN, LSTM AND AUTOENCODERS
USING TENSORFLOW 2- CONTAINS EXERCISES
WITH SOLUTIONS AND HANDS-ON PROJECTS

Contains Exercises with solutions and Hands-on Projects

AI PUBLISHING

How to Contact Us

If you have any feedback, please let us know
by sending an email to contact@aipublishing.io.

Your feedback is immensely valued,
and we look forward to hearing from you.
It will be beneficial for us
to improve the quality of our books.

To get the Python codes and materials used in this book,
please click the link below:

www.aipublishing.io/book-deep-learning-python

The order number is required

About the Publisher

At AI Publishing Company, we have established an international learning platform specifically for young students, beginners, small enterprises, startups, and managers who are new to data sciences and artificial intelligence.

Through our interactive, coherent, and practical books and courses, we help beginners learn skills that are crucial to developing AI and data science projects.

Our courses and books range from basic introduction courses to language programming and data sciences to advanced courses for machine learning, deep learning, computer vision, big data, and much more, using programming languages like Python, R, and some data science and AI software.

AI Publishing's core focus is to enable our learners to create and try proactive solutions for digital problems by leveraging the power of AI and data sciences to the maximum extent.

Moreover, we offer specialized assistance in the form of our free online content and eBooks, providing up-to-date and useful insight into AI practices and data science subjects, along with eliminating the doubts and misconceptions about AI and programming.

Our experts have cautiously developed our online courses and kept them concise, short, and comprehensive so that you can understand everything clearly and effectively and start practicing the applications right away.

We also offer consultancy and corporate training in AI and data sciences for enterprises so that their staff can navigate through the workflow efficiently.

With AI Publishing, you can always stay closer to the innovative world of AI and data sciences.

If you are eager to learn the A to Z of AI and data sciences but have no clue where to start, AI Publishing is the finest place to go.

Please contact us by email at
contact@aipublishing.io.

AI Publishing is Looking for Authors Like You

Interested in becoming an author for AI Publishing?
Please contact us at authors@aipublishing.io.

We are working with developers and AI tech professionals just like you, to help them share their insights with the global AI and Data Science lovers. You can share all your knowledge about hot topics in AI and Data Science.

Table of Contents

Preface

§ Book Approach

The book follows a simple approach. It is divided into eight chapters. Chapter 1 provides a quick introduction to deep learning and explains the installation steps for the software that we will need to implement for the various deep learning algorithms in this book. Also, chapter 1 contains a crash course on Python. Chapter 2 explains logistic and linear regression, which is a prerequisite to deep learning.

Chapter 3 explains neural networks in Python from scratch. Chapter 4 contains an introduction to the TensorFlow Keras library. You will develop neural networks using the TensorFlow Keras library in Chapter 4. The 5th Chapter explains the convolutional neural network in detail, while the 6th Chapter explains how to use a recurrent neural network (RNN) to solve different types of sequence problems. Chapter 7 provides a brief introduction to natural language processing with deep learning. Chapter 8 contains an introduction to Autoencoder, which is a type of unsupervised deep learning technique.

In each chapter, different types of deep learning techniques have been explained theoretically, followed by practical examples. Each chapter also contains exercises that students can use to evaluate their understanding of the concepts explained in the chapter. The Python notebook for each chapter is provided in the resources. It is advised that instead of copying the code, you write the code yourself, and in case of an error, you match your code with the corresponding Python notebook, find and then correct the error. The datasets used in this book are either downloaded at runtime or are available in the *Resources/Datasets* folder.

§ Data Science and Deep Learning

Data science and deep learning are two different but interrelated concepts. Data science refers to the science of extracting and exploring data in order to find patterns that can be used for decision making at different levels. Deep learning is the process of using data to train algorithms that can be used to perform different types of classification, regression, and clustering tasks.

This book is dedicated to deep learning and explains how to perform different types of deep learning tasks via various deep learning algorithms using the TensorFlow Keras library for Python. It is suggested that you use this book for deep learning purposes only and not for data science. For the application of deep learning in data science, read this book in conjunction with dedicated books on data science.

§ Who Is This Book For?

This book explains different deep learning techniques using the TensorFlow Keras library for Python. The book is aimed ideally at absolute beginners to deep learning. Though a background in the Python programming language and feature engineering can help speed up learning, the book contains a crash course on Python programming language in the first chapter. Therefore, the only prerequisites to efficiently using this book are access to a computer with internet and basic knowledge of linear algebra and calculus. All the codes and datasets have been provided. However, to download data preparation libraries, you will need the internet.

§ How to Use This Book?

As I said earlier, the deep learning techniques and concepts taught in this book have been divided into multiple chapters. To get the best out of this book, I would suggest that you first get your feet wet with the Python programming language, especially the object-oriented programming concepts. To do so, you can take the crash course on Python in the first chapter of this book. Also, try to read the chapters of this book in order since concepts taught in subsequent chapters are based on previous chapters. In each chapter, try to first understand the theoretical concepts behind different types of deep learning techniques, and then try to execute the example code. I would again stress that rather than copying and pasting code, try to write the code yourself, and in case of any error, you can match your code with the source code provided in the book as well as in the Python notebooks in the resources. Finally, try to answer the questions asked in the exercises at the end of each chapter. The solutions to the exercises have been given at the end of the Book.

To facilitate the reading process, occasionally, the book presents three types of box-tags in different colors: Requirements, **Further Readings,** and **Hands-on Time**. Examples of these boxes are shown below.

Requirements

This box lists all requirements needed to be done before proceeding to the next topic. Generally, it works as a checklist to see if everything is ready before a tutorial.

Further Readings

Here, you will be pointed to some external reference or source that will serve as additional content about the specific **Topic** being studied. In general, it consists of packages, documentations, and cheat sheets.

Hands-on Time

Here, you will be pointed to an external file to train and test all the knowledge acquired about a **Tool** that has been studied. Generally, these files are Jupyter notebooks (.ipynb), Python (.py) files, or documents (.pdf).

The box-tag Requirements lists the steps required by the reader after reading one or more topics. **Further Readings** provides relevant references for specific topics to get to know the additional content of the topics. **Hands-on Time** points to practical tools to start working on the specified topics. Follow the instructions given in the box-tags to get a better understanding of the topics presented in this book.

About the Author

M. Usman Malik holds a Ph.D. in Computer Science from Normandy University, France, with Artificial Intelligence and Machine Learning being his main areas of research. Muhammad Usman Malik has over five years of industry experience in Data Science and has worked with both private and public sector organizations. In his leisure time, he likes to listen to music and play snooker.

An Important Note to Our Valued Readers:

Download the Color Images

Our print edition books are available only in black & white at present. However, the digital edition of our books is available in color PDF.

We request you to download the PDF file containing the color images of the screenshots/diagrams used in this book here:

www.aipublishing.io/book-deep-learning-python

The typesetting and publishing costs for a color edition are prohibitive. These costs would push the final price of each book to $50, which would make the book less accessible for most beginners.

We are a small company, and we are negotiating with major publishers for a reduction in the publishing price. We are hopeful of a positive outcome sometime soon. In the meantime, we request you to help us with your wholehearted support, feedback, and review.

For the present, we have decided to print all of our books in black & white and provide access to the color version in PDF. This is a decision that would benefit the majority of our readers, as most of them are students. This would also allow beginners to afford our books.

Get in Touch With Us

Feedback from our readers is always welcome.

For general feedback, please send us an email at contact@aipublishing.io and mention the book title in the subject line.

Although we have taken extraordinary care to ensure the accuracy of our content, errors do occur. If you have found an error in this book, we would be grateful if you could report this to us as soon as you can.

If you are interested in becoming an AI Publishing author and if you have expertise in a topic and you are interested in either writing or contributing to a book, please send us an email at author@aipublishing.io.

Warning

In Python, indentation is very important. Python indentation is a way of telling a Python interpreter that the group of statements belongs to a particular code block. After each loop or if-condition, be sure to pay close attention to the intent.

§ Example

```python
# Python program showing
# indentation

site = 'aisciences'

if site == 'aisciences':
    print('Logging to www.aisciences.io...')
else:
    print('retype the URL.')
print('All set !')
```

To avoid problems during execution, we advise you to download the codes available on Github by requesting access from the link below. Please have your order number ready for access:

www.aipublishing.io/book-deep-learning-python

1

Introduction

1.1. What is Deep Learning?

With the huge amount of data at disposal, more and more researchers and industry professionals are finding ways to use this data for research and commercial benefits. Machine learning and deep learning researchers are probably the biggest beneficiaries of the availability of the huge amount of data and high-performance computing hardware.

The term deep learning is often used interchangeably with neural networks. As a matter of fact, deep learning involves the training of supervised and unsupervised learning using deeply connected neural networks. Though neural networks have been around since the 1950s, the unavailability of high-performance computing hardware held back the research and development in the domain of machine learning. It has been only possible after 2010 that deep learning algorithms have become ubiquitous.

Deep learning applications are now being used in all walks of life. From Alexa to Siri and autonomous cars to household help robots, almost all of the latest technologies involve some sort of AI. After finishing this book, you will also be equipped with enough knowledge to develop very simple deep learning applications.

In this chapter, you will see how to set up the Python environment needed to run various data deep learning. The chapter also contains a crash Python course for absolute beginners in Python. Finally, an overview of different libraries related to deep learning has been presented.

1.2. Environment Setup

1.2.1. Windows Setup

The time has come to install Python on Windows using an IDE. In fact, we will use Anaconda throughout this book right from installing Python to writing multi-threaded codes in the coming lectures. Now, let us get going with the installation.

This section explains how you can download and install Anaconda on Windows.

Download and install Anaconda by following these steps.

1. Open the following URL in your browser.

   https://www.anaconda.com/distribution/

2. The browser will take you to the following webpage. Select the latest version of Python (3.7 at the time of writing this book). Now, click the *Download* button to download the executable file. Depending upon the internet speed, the file will download within 2–3 minutes.

Windows | macOS | Linux

Anaconda 2019.07 for Windows Installer

Python 3.7 version

Download

64-Bit Graphical Installer (486 MB)
32-Bit Graphical Installer (418 MB)

Python 2.7 version

Download

64-Bit Graphical Installer (427 MB)
32-Bit Graphical Installer (361 MB)

3. Run the executable file after the download is complete. You will most likely find the download file in your download folder. The file name should be along these lines: "Anaconda3-5.1.0-Windows-x86_64." The installation wizard will open when you run the file, as shown in the following figure. Click the *Next* button.

Anaconda3 5.1.0 (64-bit) Setup   —   □   ✕

ANACONDA.

Welcome to Anaconda3 5.1.0 (64-bit) Setup

Setup will guide you through the installation of Anaconda3 5.1.0 (64-bit).

It is recommended that you close all other applications before starting Setup. This will make it possible to update relevant system files without having to reboot your computer.

Click Next to continue.

Next >   Cancel

4. Now click *I Agree* on the *License Agreement* dialog, as shown in the following screenshot.

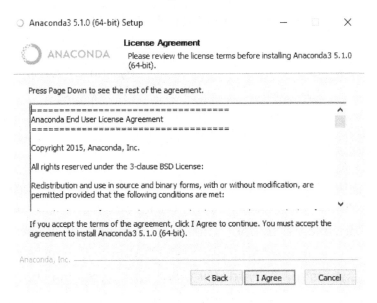

5. Check the *Just Me* radio button from the *Select Installation Type* dialogue box. Click the *Next* button to continue.

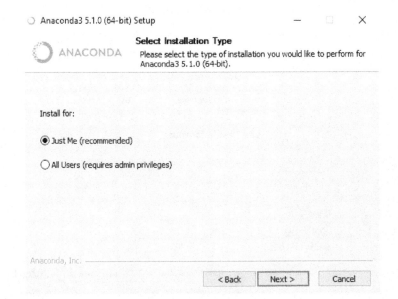

6. Now, the *Choose Install Location* dialog will be displayed. Change the directory if you want, but the default is preferred. The installation folder should at least have 3 GB of free space for Anaconda. Click the *Next* button.

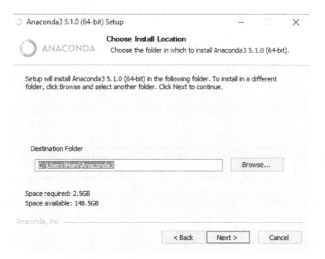

7. Go for the second option, *Register Anaconda as my default Python 3.7* in the *Advanced Installation Options* dialogue box. Click the *Install* button. The installation starts. However, this can take some time to complete.

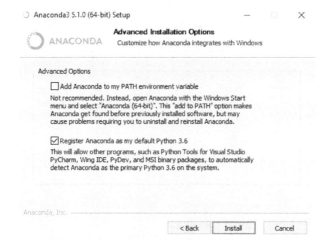

8. Click *Next* once the installation is complete.

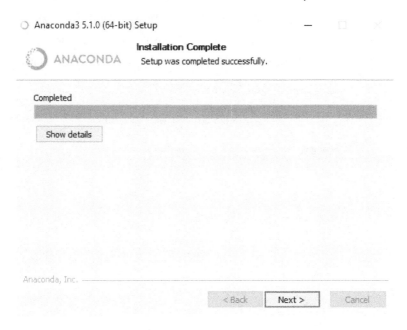

9. Click Skip on the *Microsoft Visual Studio Code Installation* dialog box.

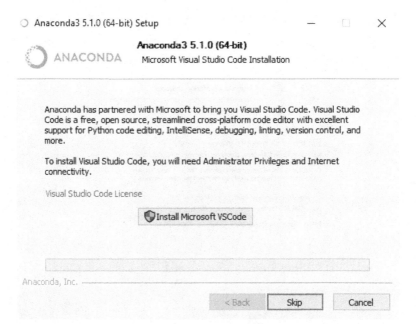

10. You have successfully installed Anaconda on your Windows. Excellent job. The next step is to uncheck both checkboxes on the dialog box. Now, click on the *Finish* button.

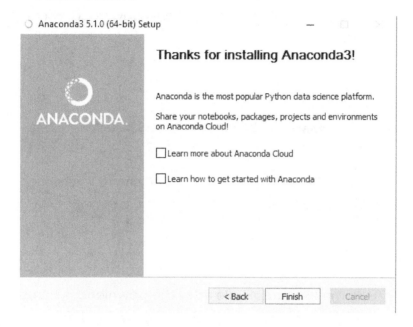

1.2.2. Mac Setup

Anaconda's installation process is almost the same for Mac. It may differ graphically, but you will follow the same steps you followed for Windows. The only difference is that you have to download the executable file, which is compatible with the Mac operating system.

This section explains how you can download and install Anaconda on Mac.

Download and install Anaconda by following these steps.

1. Open the following URL in your browser.

   https://www.anaconda.com/distribution/

2. The browser will take you to the following webpage. Select the latest version of Python for Mac. (3.7 at the time of writing this book). Now, click the *Download* button to download the executable file. Depending on the internet speed, the file will download within 2–3 minutes.

3. Run the executable file after the download is complete. You will most likely find the download file in your download folder. The name of the file should be similar to "Anaconda3-5.1.0-Windows-x86_64." The installation wizard will open when you run the file, as shown in the following figure. Click the *Continue* button.

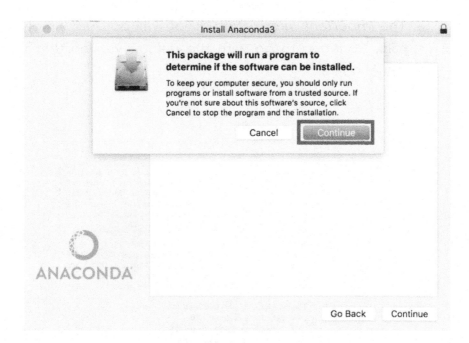

4. Now click *Continue* on the *Welcome to Anaconda 3 Installer* window, as shown in the following screenshot.

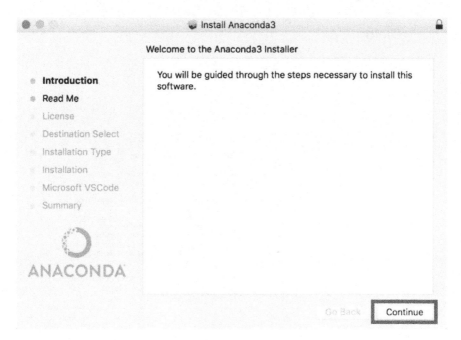

5. The *Important Information* dialog will pop up. Simply, click *Continue* to go with the default version that is Anaconda 3.

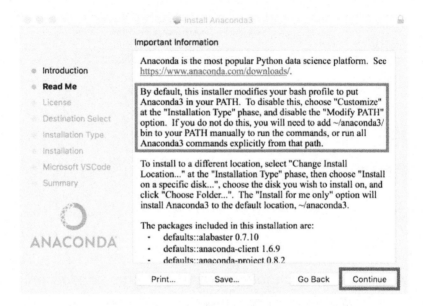

6. Click *Continue* on the *Software License Agreement* Dialog.

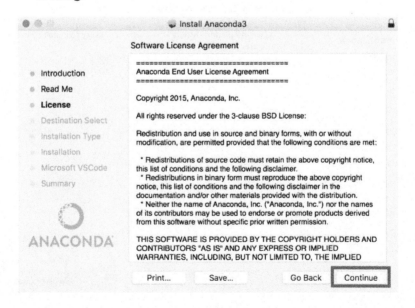

7. It is mandatory to read the license agreement and click the *Agree* button before you can click the *Continue* button again.

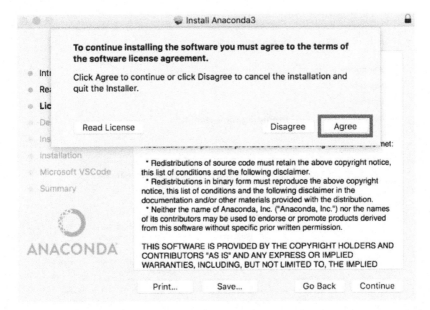

8. On the next window, simply click *Install*.

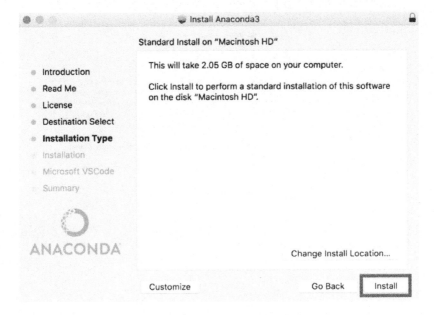

The system alerts you to give your password. Use the same password you use to login to your Mac computer. Now, click on *Install Software*.

9. Click *Continue* on the next window. You also have the option to install Microsoft VSCode at this point.

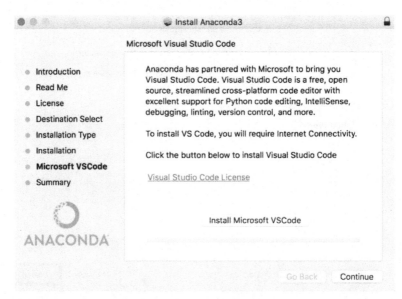

The next screen will display the message that the installation has completed successfully. Click *Close* to close the installer.

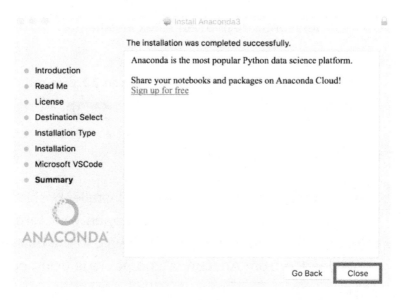

There you have it. You have successfully installed Anaconda on your Mac computer. Now, you can write Python code in Jupyter and Spyder the same way you wrote it in Windows.

1.2.3. Linux Setup

We have used Python's graphical installers for installation on Windows and Mac. However, we will use the command line to install Python on Ubuntu or Linux. Linux is also more resource-friendly, and the installation of software is particularly easy, as well.

Follow these steps to install Anaconda on Linux (Ubuntu distribution).

1. Go to the following link to copy the installer bash script from the latest available version.

   https://www.anaconda.com/distribution/

Anaconda 2019.07 for Linux Installer

Python 3.7 version

Download

64-Bit (x86) Installer (517 MB)
64-Bit (Power8 and Power9) Installer (326 MB)

Python 2.7 version

Download

64-Bit (x86) Installer (476 MB)
64-Bit (Power8 and Power9) Installer (298 MB)

2. The second step is to download the installer bash script. Log into your Linux computer and open your terminal. Now, go to /temp directory and download the bash you downloaded from Anaconda's home page using curl.

```
$ cd / tmp

$ curl -o https://repo.anaconda.com.archive/Anaconda3-5.2.0-
Linux-x86_64.sh
```

3. You should also use the cryptographic hash verification through SHA-256 checksum to verify the integrity of the installer.

```
$ sha256sum Anaconda3-5.2.0-Linux-x86_64.sh
```

You will get the following output.

```
09f53738b0cd3bb96f5b1bac488e5528df9906be2480fe61df40e0e0d19e
3d48 Anaconda3-5.2.0-Linux-x86_64.sh
```

4. The fourth step is to run the Anaconda Script, as shown in the following figure.

```
$ bash Anaconda3-5.2.0-Linux-x86_64.sh
```

The command line will produce the following output. You will be asked to review the license agreement. Keep on pressing *Enter* until you reach the end.

```
Output

Welcome to Anaconda3 5.2.0

In order to continue the installation process, please review
the license agreement.
Please, press Enter to continue
>>>
...
Do you approve the license terms? [yes|No]
```

Type Yes when you get to the bottom of the License Agreement.

5. The installer will alert you to choose the installation location after you agree to the license agreement. Simply press *Enter* to choose the default location. You can also specify a different location if you want.

```
Output

Anaconda3 will now be installed on this location:
/home/tola/anaconda3

- Press ENTER to confirm the location
- Press CTRL-C to abort the installation
- Or specify a different location below

[/home/tola/anaconda3] >>>
```

The installation will proceed once you press *Enter*. Once again, you have to be patient as the installation process takes some time to complete.

6. You will receive the following result when the installation is complete. If you wish to use conda command, type *Yes*.

```
Output
...
Installation finished.
Do you wish the installer to prepend Anaconda3 install
location to path in your /home/tola/.bashrc? [yes|no]
[no]>>>
```

At this point, you will also have the option to download the Visual Studio Code. Type *yes* or *no* to install or decline, respectively.

7. Use the following command to activate your brand-new installation of Anaconda3.

```
$ source `/.bashrc
```

8. You can also test the installation using the conda command.

```
$ conda list
```

Congratulations. You have successfully installed Anaconda on your Linux system.

1.2.4. Using Google Colab Cloud Environment

In addition to local Python environments such as Anaconda, you can run deep learning applications on Google Colab as well, which is Google's platform for deep learning with GPU support. All the codes in this book have been run using Google Colab. Therefore, I would suggest that you use Google Colab too.

To run deep learning applications via Google Colab, all you need is a Google/Gmail account. Once you have a Google/Gmail account, you can simply go to:

https://colab.research.google.com/

Next, click on File -> New notebook, as shown in the following screenshot.

Next, to run your code using GPU, from the top menu, select Runtime -> Change runtime type as shown in the following screenshot:

Runtime	Tools	Help	Last edited on M
Run all			Ctrl+F9
Run before			Ctrl+F8
Run the focused cell			Ctrl+Enter
Run selection			Ctrl+Shift+Enter
Run after			Ctrl+F10

Factory reset runtime

Change runtime type

Manage sessions

You should see the following window. Here from the dropdown list, select GPU, and click the *Save* button.

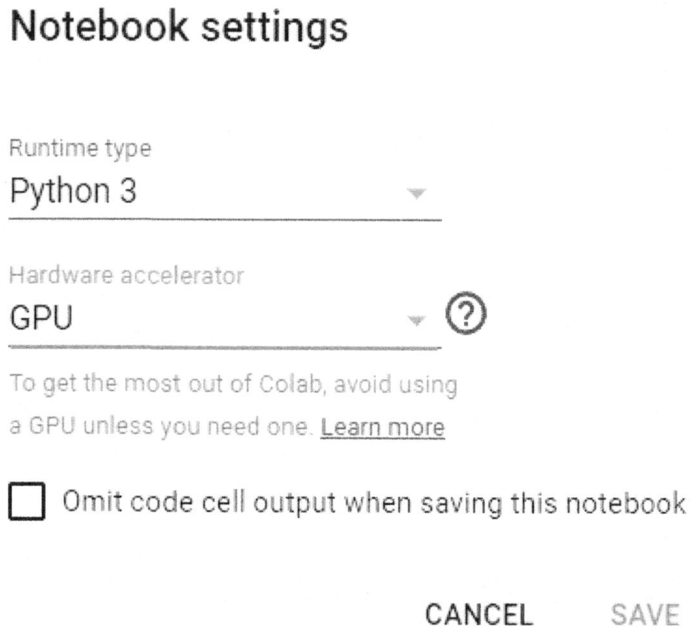

Notebook settings

Runtime type

Python 3 ▾

Hardware accelerator

GPU ▾ ⑦

To get the most out of Colab, avoid using a GPU unless you need one. Learn more

☐ Omit code cell output when saving this notebook

CANCEL   SAVE

To make sure you are running the latest version of TensorFlow, execute the following script in the Google Colab notebook cell. The following script will update your TensorFlow version.

```
pip install --upgrade tensorflow
```

To check if you are really running TensorFlow version > 2.0, execute the following script.

```
import tensorflow as tf
print(tf.__version__)
```

With Google Cloud, you can import the datasets from your Google drive. Execute the following script, and click on the link that appears as shown below:

```
from google.colab import drive
drive.mount('/gdrive')

Go to this URL in a browser: https://accounts.google.com/o/oauth2/auth

Enter your authorization code:
```

You will be prompted to allow Google Colab to access your Google drive. Click *Allow* button as shown below:

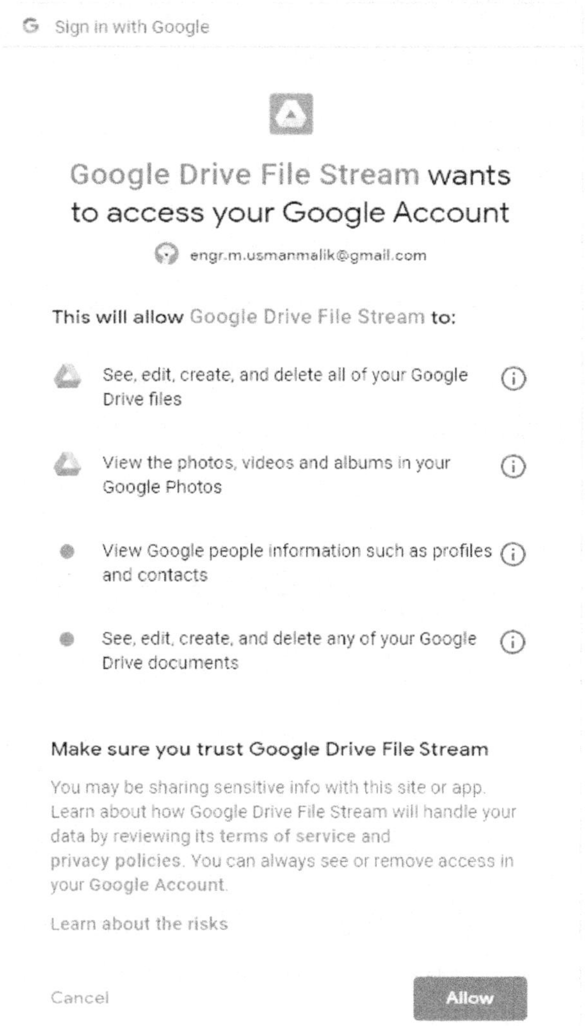

G Sign in with Google

Google Drive File Stream wants to access your Google Account

engr.m.usmanmalik@gmail.com

This will allow Google Drive File Stream **to:**

See, edit, create, and delete all of your Google Drive files

View the photos, videos and albums in your Google Photos

View Google people information such as profiles and contacts

See, edit, create, and delete any of your Google Drive documents

Make sure you trust Google Drive File Stream

You may be sharing sensitive info with this site or app. Learn about how Google Drive File Stream will handle your data by reviewing its terms of service and privacy policies. You can always see or remove access in your Google Account.

Learn about the risks

Cancel   Allow

You will see a link appear, as shown in the following image (the link has been blinded here).

Google

Sign in

Please copy this code, switch to your application and paste it there:

cIjiqzw

Copy this link. Paste it in the field in the Google Colab cell, as shown below:

```
from google.colab import drive
drive.mount('/gdrive')

Go to this URL in a browser: https://accounts.google.com/o/oauth2/auth

Enter your authorization code:
```

1.3. Python Crash Course

If you are familiar with the foundational concepts of the Python programming language, you can skip this section. For those who are absolute beginners to Python, this section provides a very brief overview of some of the most basic concepts of Python. Python is a very vast programming language, and this section is by no means a substitute for a complete Python Book. However, if you want to see how various operations and commands are executed in Python, you are welcome to follow along the rest of this section.

1.3.1. Writing Your First Program

The installation of Python on your computer is complete. You have established a unique environment in the form of Anaconda. Now, it is time to write your first program, that is the Hello World!

In order to write a program in Anaconda, you have to launch Anaconda Navigator. Search *Anaconda Navigator* in your Windows Search Box. Now, click on the Anaconda Navigator application icon, as shown in the following figure.

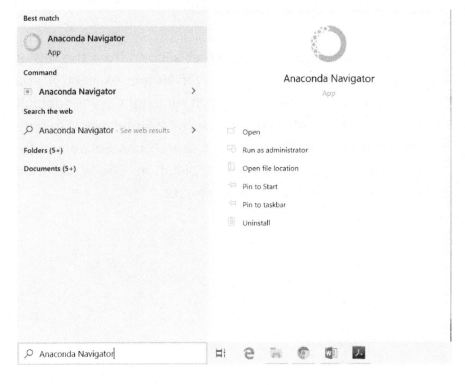

Once you click on the application, the Anaconda's Dashboard will open. The Dashboard offers you a myriad of tools to write your code. We will use the *Jupyter Notebook*, the most popular of these tools, to write and explain the code throughout this book.

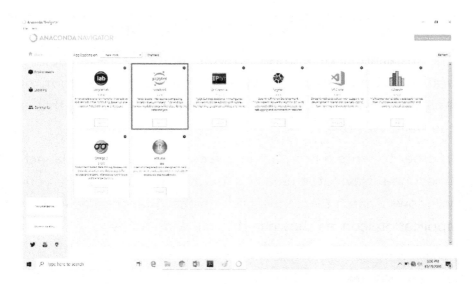

The Jupyter Notebook is available at second from the top of the Dashboard. You can use Jupyter Notebook even if you don't have access to the internet as it runs right in your default browser. Another method to open Jupyter Notebook is to type *Jupyter Notebook* in the Windows search bar. Subsequently, click on the Jupyter Notebook application. The application will open in the new tab of your browser.

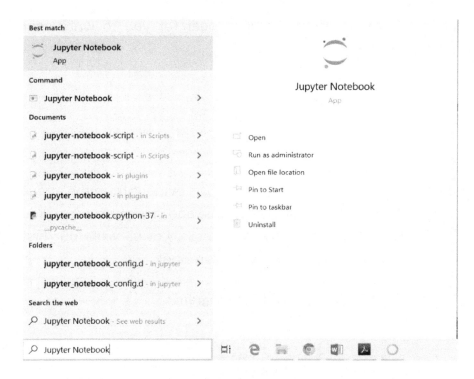

The top right corner of Jupyter Notebook's own Dashboard houses a *New* button, which you have to click to open a new document. A dropdown containing several options will appear. Click on *Python 3*.

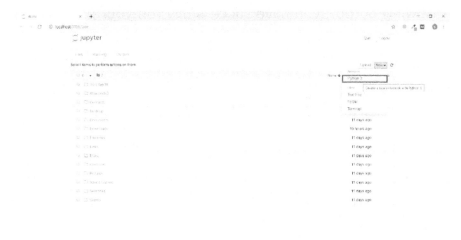

A new Python notebook will appear for you to write your programs. It looks as follows.

Jupyter Notebook consists of cells, as evident from the above image, making its layout very simple and straightforward. You will write your code inside these cells. Let us write our first ever Python program in Jupyter Notebook.

1.3.1. Writing Your First Program

```
In [1]:  print("Welcome to Data Visualization with Python")

         Welcome to Data Visualization with Python
```

The above script basically prints a string value in the output using the **print()** method. The **print()** method is used to print on the console, any string passed to it. If you see the following output, you have successfully run your first Python program.

Output:

```
Welcome to Data Visualization with Python
```

Let's now explore some of the other important Python concepts starting with Variables and Data Types.

Requirements – Anaconda, Jupyter

- All the scripts in this book have been executed via Jupyter notebook. Therefore, you should have Jupyter notebook installed.

Hands-on Time – Source Codes

All IPython notebook for the source code of all the scripts in this chapter can be found in Resources/Source Codes/ Chapter 1.ipynb. I would suggest that you write all the code in this chapter yourself and see if you can get the same output as mentioned in this chapter.

1.3.2. Python Variables and Data Types

Data types in a programming language refers to the type of data that the language is capable of processing. The following are the major data types supported by Python.

a. Strings

b. Integers

c. Floating Point Numbers

d. Booleans

e. Lists

f. Tuples

g. Dictionaries

A variable is an alias for the memory address where actual data is stored. The data or the values stored at a memory address can be accessed and updated via the variable name. Unlike other programming languages like C++, Java, and C#, Python is loosely typed, which means that you don't have to define the data type while creating a variable. Rather, the type of data is evaluated at runtime.

The following example demonstrates how to create different data types and how to store them in their corresponding variables. The script also prints the type of the variables via the **type()** function.

Script 2:

```
1.   # A string Variable
2.   first_name = "Joseph"
3.   print(type(first_name))
4.
5.   # An Integer Variable
6.   age = 20
7.   print(type(age))
8.
9.   # A floating point variable
10.  weight = 70.35
11.  print(type(weight))
12.
13.  # A boolean variable
14.  married = False
15.  print(type(married))
16.
17.  #List
18.  cars = ["Honda", "Toyota", "Suzuki"]
19.  print(type(cars))
20.
21.  #Tuples
22.  days = ("Sunday", "Monday", "Tuesday", "Wednesday",
         "Thursday", "Friday", "Saturday")
23.  print(type(days))
24.
25.  #Dictionaries
26.  days2 = {1:"Sunday", 2:"Monday", 3:"Tuesday",
         4:"Wednesday", 5:"Thursday", 6:"Friday", 7:"Saturday"}
27.  print(type(days2))
```

Output:

```
<class 'str'>
<class 'int'>
<class 'float'>
<class 'bool'>
<class 'list'>
<class 'tuple'>
<class 'dict'>
```

1.3.3. Python Operators

Python programming language contains the following types of operators:

a. Arithmetic Operators

b. Logical Operators

c. Comparison Operators

d. Assignment Operators

e. Membership Operators

Let's briefly review each of these types of operators.

Arithmetic Operators

These operators are used to execute arithmetic operations in Python. The following table sums up the arithmetic operators supported by Python. Suppose X = 20 and Y = 10.

Operator Name	Symbol	Functionality	Example
Addition	+	Adds the operands on either side	X+ Y= 30
Subtraction	-	Subtracts the operands on either side	X -Y= 10
Multiplication	*	Multiplies the operands on either side	X * Y= 200
Division	/	Divides the operand on left by the one on right	X / Y= 2.0
Modulus	%	Divides the operand on left by the one on right and returns remainder	X % Y= 0
Exponent	**	Takes exponent of the operand on the left to the power of right	X ** Y = $1024 \times e^{10}$

Here is an example of arithmetic operators with output:

Script 3:

```
1.  X = 20
2.  Y = 10
3.  print(X + Y)
4.  print(X - Y)
5.  print(X * Y)
6.  print(X / Y)
7.  print(X ** Y)
```

Output:

```
30
10
200
2.0
10240000000000
```

Logical Operators

Logical operators are used to perform logical **AND,** **OR**, and **NOT** operations in Python. The following table summarizes the logical operators. Here **X** is **True**, and **Y** is **False**.

Operator	Symbol	Functionality	Example
Logical AND	and	If both the operands are truethen condition becomestrue.	(X and Y) = False
Logical OR	or	If any of the twooperands are truethen condition becomestrue.	(X or Y) = True
Logical NOT	not	Used to reverse the logical state of itsoperand.	not(X and Y) =True

Here is an example that explains the usage of Python logical operators.

Script 4:

```
1.  X = True
2.  Y = False
3.  print(X and Y)
4.  print(X or Y)
5.  print(not(X and Y))
```

Output:

```
1.  False
2.  True
3.  True
```

Comparison Operators

Comparison operators, as the name suggests, are used to compare two or more than two operands. Depending upon the relation between the operands, comparison operators return

Boolean values. The following table summarizes comparison operators in Python. Here, X is 20, and Y is 35.

Operator	Symbol	Description	Example
Equality	==	Returns true if values of both the operands are equal	(X == Y) = false
Inequality	!=	Returns true if values of both the operands are not equal	(X = Y) = true
Greater than	>	Returns true if value of the left operand is greater than the right one	(X> Y) = False
Smaller than	<	Returns true if value of the left operand is smaller than the right one	(X< Y) = True
Greater than or equal to	>=	Returns true if value of the left operand is greater than or equal to the right one	(X > =Y) = False
Smaller than or equal to	<=	Returns true if value of the left operand is smaller than or equal to the right one	(X<= Y) = True

The comparison operators have been demonstrated in action in the following example:

Script 5

```
1.  X = 20
2.  Y = 35
3.
4.  print(X == Y)
5.  print(X != Y)
6.  print(X > Y)
7.  print(X < Y)
8.  print(X >= Y)
9.  print(X <= Y)
```

Output:

```
False
True
False
True
False
True
```

Assignment Operators

These operators are used to assign values to variables. The following table summarizes the assignment operators. Here, X is 20, and Y is equal to 10.

Operator	Symbol	Description	Example
Assignment	=	Used to assign value of the right operand to the one on the left	R = X+ Y assigns 30 to R
Add and assign	+=	Adds the operands on either side and assigns the result to the left operand	X += Y assigns 30 to X
Subtract and assign	-=	Subtracts the operands on either side and assigns the result to the left operand	X -= Y assigns 10 to X
Multiply and Assign	*=	Multiplies the operands on either side and assigns the result to the left operand	X *= Y assigns 200 to X
Divide and Assign	/=	Divides the operands on the left by the right and assigns the result to the left operand	X/= Y assigns 2 to X

Take modulus and assign	%=	Divides the operands on the left by the right and assigns the remainder to the left operand	X %= Y assigns 0 to X
Take exponent and assign	**=	Takes the exponent of the operand on the left to the power of right and assign the remainder to the left operand	X **= Y assigns 1024 x e^{10} to X

Take a look at script 6 to see Python assignment operators in action.

Script 6:

```
1.  X = 20; Y = 10
2.  R = X + Y
3.  print(R)
4.
5.  X = 20;
6.  Y = 10
7.  X += Y
8.  print(X)
9.
10. X = 20;
11. Y = 10
12. X -= Y
13. print(X)
14.
15. X = 20;
16. Y = 10
17. X *= Y
18. print(X)
19.
20. X = 20;
21. Y = 10
22. X /= Y
23. print(X)
24.
```

```
25. X = 20;
26. Y = 10
27. X %= Y
28. print(X)
29.
30. X = 20;
31. Y = 10
32. X **= Y
33. print(X)
```

Output:

```
30
30
10
200
2.0
0
10240000000000
```

Membership Operators

Membership operators are used to find if an item is a member of a collection of items or not. There are two types of membership operators—the **in** operator and the **not in** operator. The following script shows **in** operator in action.

Script 7:

```
1.  days = ("Sunday", "Monday", "Tuesday", "Wednesday",
        "Thursday", "Friday", "Saturday")
2.  print('Sunday' in days)
```

Output:

```
True
```

And here is an example of the **not in** operator.

Script 8:

```
1.  days = ("Sunday", "Monday", "Tuesday", "Wednesday",
        "Thursday", "Friday", "Saturday")
2.  print('Xunday' not in days)
```

Output:

```
True
```

1.3.4. Conditional Statements

Conditional statements in Python are used to implement conditional logic in Python. Conditional statements help you decide whether to execute a certain code block or not. There are three chief types of conditional statements in Python:

    a. If statement

    b. If-else statement

    c. If-elif statement

IF Statement

If you have to check for a single condition and you do not concern about the alternate condition, you can use the **if** statement. For instance, if you want to check if 10 is greater than 5 and based on that you want to print a statement, you can use the if statement. The condition evaluated by the **if** statement returns a Boolean value. If the condition evaluated by the **if** statement is true, the code block that follows the **if** statement executes. It is important to mention that in Python, a new code block starts at a new line with on tab indented from the left when compared with the outer block.

Here in the following example, the condition 10 > 5 is evaluated, which returns true. Hence, the code block that follows the **if** statement executes, and a message is printed on the console.

Script 8:

```
1.   # The if statment
2.
3.   if 10 > 5:
4.       print("Ten is greater than 10")
```

Output:

```
Ten is greater than 10
```

IF-Else Statement

The **If-else** statement comes handy when you want to execute an alternate piece of code in case the condition for the if statement returns false. For instance, in the following example, the condition 5 < 10 will return false. Hence, the code block that follows the **else** statement will execute.

Script 9:

```
1.   # if-else statement
2.
3.   if  5 > 10:
4.       print("5 is greater than 10")
5.   else:
6.       print("10 is greater than 5")
```

Output:

```
10 is greater than 5
```

IF-Elif Statement

The **if-elif** statement comes handy when you have to evaluate multiple conditions. For instance, in the following example, we first check if 5 > 10, which evaluates to false. Next, an **elif** statement evaluates the condition 8 < 4, which also returns false. Hence, the code block that follows the last **else** statement executes.

Script 10:

```
1.  #if-elif and else
2.
3.  if  5 > 10:
4.      print("5 is greater than 10")
5.  elif 8 < 4:
6.      print("8 is smaller than 4")
7.  else:
8.      print("5 is not greater than 10 and 8 is not smaller
    than 4")
```

Output:

```
5 is not greater than 10 and 8 is not smaller than 4
```

1.3.5. Iteration Statements

Iteration statements, also known as loops, are used to iteratively execute a certain piece of code. There are two main types of iteration statements in Python.

    a. For loop

    b. While Loop

For Loop

The **for loop** is used to iteratively execute a piece of code for a certain number of times. You should use **for loop** when you exactly know the number of iterations or repetitions for which you want to run your code. A **for loop** iterates over a collection of items. In the following example, we create a collection of five integers using **range()** method. Next, a **for loop** iterates five times and prints each integer in the collection.

Script 11:

```
1.  items = range(5)
2.  for item in items:
3.      print(item)
```

Output:

```
0
1
2
3
4
```

While Loop

The **while loop** keeps executing a certain piece of code unless the evaluation condition becomes false. For instance, the **while loop** in the following script keeps executing unless variable c becomes greater than 10.

Script 12:

```
1.   c = 0
2.   while c < 10:
3.       print(c)
4.       c = c +1
```

Output:

```
0
1
2
3
4
5
6
7
8
9
```

1.3.6. Functions

In any programming language, functions are used to implement the piece of code that is required to be executed numerous times at different locations in the code. In such cases, instead of writing long pieces of codes again and again, you can simply define a function that contains the piece of code, and then you can call the function wherever you want in the code.

To create a function in Python, the def keyword is used, followed by the name of the function and opening and closing parenthesis.

Once a function is defined, you have to call it in order to execute the code inside a function body. To call a function, you simply have to specify the name of the function, followed by opening and closing parenthesis. In the following script, we create a function named **myfunc**, which prints a simple statement on the console using the **print()** method.

Script 13:

```
1.   def myfunc():
2.       print("This is a simple function")
3.
4.   ### function call
5.   myfunc()
```

Output:

```
This is a simple function
```

You can also pass values to a function. The values are passed inside the parenthesis of the function call. However, you must specify the parameter name in the function definition, too. In the following script, we define a function named **myfuncparam()**. The function accepts one parameter, i.e. **num**. The value passed in the parenthesis of the function call will be stored in this **num** variable and will be printed by the **print()**method inside the **myfuncparam()** method.

Script 14:

```
1.   def myfuncparam(num):
2.       print("This is a function with parameter value: "+num)
3.
4.   ### function call
5.   myfuncparam("Parameter 1")
```

Output:

```
This is a function with parameter value:Parameter 1
```

Finally, a function can also return values to the function call. To do so, you simply have to use the return keyword, followed by the value that you want to return. In the following script, the **myreturnfunc()** function returns a string value to the calling function.

Script 15:

```
1.   def myreturnfunc():
2.       return "This function returns a value"
3.
4.   val = myreturnfunc()
5.   print(val)
```

Output:

```
This function returns a value
```

1.3.7. Objects and Classes

Python supports object-oriented programming (OOP). In OOP, any entity that can perform some function and have some attributes is implemented in the form of an object.

For instance, a car can be implemented as an object since a car has some attributes such as price, color, and model, and can perform some functions such as drive car, change gear, stop car, etc.

Similarly, a fruit can also be implemented as an object since a fruit has a price, name, and you can eat a fruit, grow a fruit, and perform functions with a fruit.

To create an object, you first have to define a class. For instance, in the following example, a class **Fruit** has been defined. The class has two attributes **name** and **price**, and one method **eat_fruit()**. Next, we create an object **f** of class Fruit and then call the **eat_fruit()** method from the **f** object. We also access the **name** and **price** attributes of the **f** object and print them on the console.

Script 16:

```
1.    class Fruit:
2.
3.        name = "apple"
4.        price = 10
5.
6.        def eat_fruit(self):
7.            print("Fruit has been eaten")
8.
9.
10.   f = Fruit()
11.   f.eat_fruit()
12.   print(f.name)
13.   print(f.price)
```

Output:

```
Fruit has been eaten
apple
10
```

A class in Python can have a special method called a constructor. The name of the constructor method in Python is **__init__()**. The constructor is called whenever an object of a class is created. Look at the following example to see a constructor in action.

Script 17:

```
1.  class Fruit:
2.
3.      name = "apple"
4.      price = 10
5.
6.      def __init__(self, fruit_name, fruit_price):
7.          Fruit.name = fruit_name
8.          Fruit.price = fruit_price
9.
10.     def eat_fruit(self):
11.         print("Fruit has been eaten")
12.
13.
14. f = Fruit("Orange", 15)
15. f.eat_fruit()
16. print(f.name)
17. print(f.price)
```

Output:

```
Fruit has been eaten
Orange
15
```

Further Readings – Python [1]

To study more about Python, please check Python 3 Official Documentation. Get used to searching and reading this documentation. It is a great resource of knowledge.

1.4. Some Useful Libraries for Deep Learning

Owing to the boom of deep learning applications, various deep learning libraries have been developed in order to expedite the research and development in the field of deep learning and AI. Some of these libraries have been presented in the next section.

1.4.1. TensorFlow

TensorFlow is one of the most commonly used libraries for deep learning. TensorFlow has been developed by Google and offers an easy to use API for the development of various deep learning models. TensorFlow is consistently being updated, and at the time of writing of this book, TensorFlow 2 is the latest major release of TensorFlow. With TensorFlow, you can not only easily develop deep learning applications but also deploy them with ease owing to the deployment functionalities of TensorFlow.

1.4.2. Keras

Keras is a high-level TensorFlow library that implements complex TensorFlow functionalities under the hood. If you are new to deep learning, Keras is the one deep learning library that you should start with for developing deep learning library. As a matter of fact, Keras has been adopted as the official deep learning library for TensorFlow 2.0, and now all the TensorFlow applications use Keras abstractions for training deep learning models.

1.4.3. Pytorch

Pytorch is another famous and probably the only competitor deep learning library to TensorFlow and Keras. Pytorch is developed by Facebook and offers a high-level abstraction to various deep learning models. However, in this book, we will not be using Pytorch. Rather, we will be working with TensorFlow and Keras.

1.4.4. NumPy

NumPy is one of the most commonly used libraries for numeric and scientific computing. NumPy is extremely fast and contains support for multiple mathematical domains such as linear algebra, geometry, etc. It is extremely important to learn NumPy in case you plan to make a career in data science and data preparation.

1.4.5. Scikit Learn

Scikit Learn, also called sklearn, is an extremely useful library for machine learning in Python. Sklearn contains many built-in modules that can be used to perform data preparation tasks such as feature engineering, feature scaling, outlier detection, discretization, etc. You will be using Sklearn a lot in this book. Therefore, it can be a splendid idea to study sklearn before you start coding using this book.

1.4.6. Matplotlib

Data visualization is an important precursor to data preparation. Before you actually apply data preparation techniques on the data, you should know how the data looks like, what is the distribution of a certain variable, etc. Matplotlib is the de facto standard for static data visualization in Python.

1.4.7. Seaborn

Seaborn library is built on top of the Matplotlib library and contains all the plotting capabilities of Matplotlib. However, with Seaborn, you can plot much more pleasing and aesthetic graphs with the help of Seaborn default styles and color palettes.

1.4.8. Pandas

Pandas library, like Seaborn, is based on the Matplotlib library and offers utilities that can be used to plot different types of static plots in a single line of codes. With Pandas, you can import data in various formats such as CSV (Comma Separated View) and TSV (Tab Separated View) and can plot a variety of data visualizations via these data sources.

Further Readings – Data Preparation Libraries

To study more about data preparation libraries for Python, check these links:
Numpy [1], Scikit Learn [2], Matplotlib [3], Seaborn [4], and Pandas [5]

---

§ References

1. https://numpy.org/

2. https://scikit-learn.org/

3. https://matplotlib.org/

4. https://seaborn.pydata.org/index.html

5. https://pandas.pydata.org/

Exercise 1.1

Question 1

Which iteration should be used when you want to repeatedly execute a code a specific number of times?

1. For Loop
2. While Loop
3. Both A and B
4. None of the above

Question 2

What is the maximum number of values that a function can return in Python?

1. Single Value
2. Double Value
3. More than two values
4. None

Question 3

Which of the following membership operators are supported by Python?

1. In
2. Out
3. Not In
4. Both A and C

Exercise 1.2

Print the table of integer for 9 using a while loop.

2

Deep Learning Prerequisites: Linear and Logistic Regression

Before we go on and study neural networks in detail in Chapter 3, it is important to understand linear and logistic regression because, effectively, a densely connected neural network is a combination of multiple linear or logistic regression units.

In this chapter, you will see how to implement univariate and multivariate linear regression from scratch in Python. You will also see how you can extend the linear regression model to implement logistic regression. You will also see how to derive the equations involved to implement linear and logistic regressions in Python.

2.1. Linear Regression

Linear regression is a mathematical approach to find the relationship between two or more than two input variables with a target variable. Linear regression assumes that there is a linear relationship between the input and the target variable. A simple example of a linear relationship can be the relation between the height and weight of a person. A taller person is heavier than a shorter person with the same body mass index. Similarly, the price of a car goes up with the model. Newer cars of the same model are expensive compared to older cars.

If you plot the relationship between two variables that are linearly related, you should see a line identical to the one in the following image.

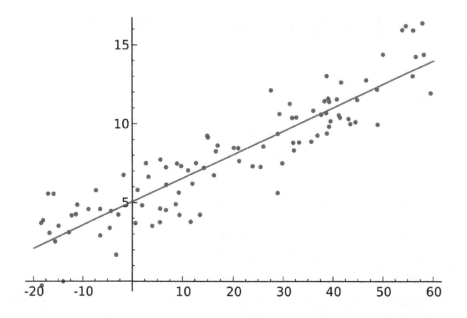

The variables in the above line are positively correlated. The increase in variables on the x-axis causes an increase in the value of the variables on the y-axis. If the variables are negatively linearly related, you should see a straight line going downward from left to right.

It is important to mention that in linear regression, the output is a continuous number, which means that you can use linear regression to solve problems like house price prediction, person weight prediction, and so on and so forth.

Linear regression can be of two types: univariate linear regression and multivariate linear regression.

2.1.1. Univariate Linear Regression

In univariate linear regression, you have to find the relationship between one input variable and one target variable. Linear regression between one input and one target variable can be represented by a straight line. In other words, you have to find a straight line that passes through all the points that are used to demonstrate a relationship between input and target variables.

The question here is, how we can find the best line because there can be multiple lines that can pass through the points. The best line is, therefore, the one that minimizes the errors between the actual data points and the predicted data points. Look at the following figure. Here, the blue line is our regression line, and the red points are the actual data points. We have to find a line such that the distance between the line and red points is minimized. The sum of the square of all the distances between the line and points is called error or cost. Our target is to minimize costs. In the next section, you will see how we can do that mathematically.

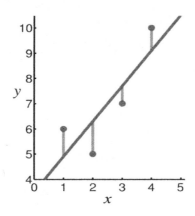

From algebra, we know that the equation of a straight line is:

y = ax + b ---------------- (1)

Equation 1: Equation of a Straight line

Where ax is the slope of the line, and b is the point where the line intercepts the y-coordinate. Here, x refers to the input data, and y represents the outputs. We do not have any control over x and y. The only thing we can control is the value of the variables a and b. The idea is to find those values of a and b that give us a line or slope, which minimizes the distance between the line and the actual data points. In other words, we need to minimize the error.

The Cost Function

As a first step, let's write a function that finds the error. There are several error functions, but the most commonly used error function for linear regression is mean squared error, which can be found by calculating the sum of squares of the differences between the values predicted by our equation (slope) and the actual values. The following function shows how to find the error or cost:

$$ J = \frac{1}{m} \sum_{i=1}^{m} (y^{\wedge}{}_i - y_i)^2 $$

Equation 2: Mean Squared Error Cost Function

In equation 2, y^ refers to the prediction. The prediction is actually equal to:

$$ y^{\wedge}{}_i = (ax_i + b_i) $$

Equation 3: Prediction Equation

Hence, we can replace equation 3 in equation 2 to get:

$$J = \frac{1}{m} \sum_{i=1}^{m} (ax_i + b_i - y_i)^2$$

Equation 4: Final Cost Function

We have to minimize the error. The error is given by the cost function J, which means that we have to minimize the cost function J with respect to variables a and b. Or in other words, we have to find the values for a and b for which we can find the minimum error. We can do so with the help of gradient descent function.

Gradient Descent Function

With gradient descent, you can find the minima of a function with respect to a specific input variable. An image of the gradient function is as follows:

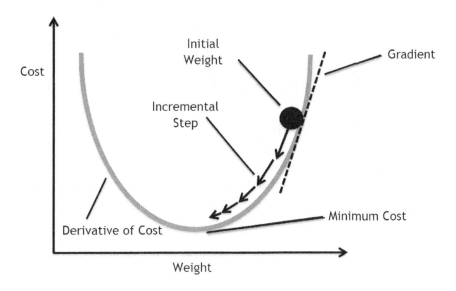

In our case, the weights are a and b.

The following are the steps involved in the gradient descent of our cost function J.

1. In gradient descent function, we will start with the arbitrary values of a and b.

2. Using those values, we will take the derivative of our cost function J with respect to the variables a and b. The derivative will tell us if the error or cost is increasing or decreasing at the current values of a and b.

3. The derivatives are subtracted from the current values of a and b. The derivatives can be multiplied by a learning rate that defines the size or jump that the variables should move downward.

Let's find the derivatives of our cost function J, with respect to variables a and b.

$$\frac{J\Delta}{J(a)} = \frac{1}{m}\sum_{i=1}^{m} 2(ax_i + b_i - y_i)(xi)$$

Equation 5: Derivative of Cost Function with Respect to the Variable a

In the above equation, you can ignore 2 because it is a constant. The derivative of cost function simply becomes the sum of all the errors multiplied by the corresponding input values, divided by the number of inputs.

The derivative of the cost function, similarly, with respect to the bias b is (b is also known as bias):

$$\frac{J\Delta}{J(b)} = \frac{1}{m}\sum_{i=1}^{m} 2(ax_i + b_i - y_i)$$

Equation 6: Derivative of Cost Function with Respect to the Variable b

The bias value here is simply the error. Again, here the constant 2 can be removed.

To implement the gradient descent, all you have to do now is repeatedly subtract $\frac{J\Delta \ J\Delta}{J(a)J(a)}$ from a, and $\frac{J\Delta \ J\Delta}{J(b)J(b)}$ from b as shown in the following equations:

$$a = a - lr * \frac{J\Delta}{J(a)}$$

Equation 7: Gradient Descent Equation for Variable a

$$b = a - lr * \frac{J\Delta}{J(b)}$$

Equation 8: Gradient Descent Equation for variable b

In the next section, you will see the implementation of linear regression from scratch in Python.

Implementing Univariate Linear Regression from Scratch in Python

Let's first create a dummy regression dataset with 1 feature and 1 target variable.

Script 1:

```
1.  from sklearn.datasets import make_regression
2.  import matplotlib.pyplot as plt
3.  import numpy as np
4.
5.  X, y= make_regression(n_samples=100, n_features=1,
    noise=1.0, bias=50)
6.  y = y.reshape(y.shape[0],1)
```

The following script plots the relationship between the input variable X and the target variable y.

Script 2:

```
1.    plt.scatter(X,y)
2.    plt.rcParams["figure.figsize"] = [8 , 6]
```

Output:

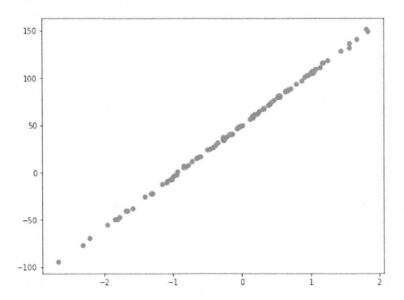

The above output shows that the variables X and y are linearly related since the output is in the form of a straight line.

Let's check the shape of our dataset.

Script 3:

```
1.    print(X.shape)
2.    print(y.shape)
```

Output:

```
(100, 1)
(100, 1)
```

Our input feature set consists of 100 rows and 1 column. The output label has the same dimensions.

Let's now create a function that returns the weights for our algorithm. Remember, a and b are basically weights for our regression algorithm.

Script 4:

```
1.   def define_parameters(n_weights):
2.       a = np.random.randn( n_weights, 1)
3.       b = np.random.randn()
4.       return a, b
```

The following script defines a method named make predictions. This method takes the weights and the input feature set as input, performs dot product between the inputs and weights, and then adds bias to the result. The **predictions()** method returns the dot product of weights and input features plus bias. The prediction function basically implements equation 1 from the theory section.

Script 5:

```
1.   def predictions(a, b , X):
2.       z = np.dot(X,a) + b
3.       return z
```

The script below finds the cost function by implementing equation 2 from the theory section.

Script 6:

```
1.   def find_cost(z,y):
2.       m = y.shape[0]
3.       total_cost = (1/m)*np.sum(np.square(z - y))
4.       return total_cost
```

The following script implements the equations 5 and 6 from the theory section and finds the derivatives of the cost function with respect to the input variables a and b. The resultant derivative is returned to the calling function.

Script 7:

```
1.  def find_derivatives(X, y, z):
2.      m = y.shape[0]
3.      dz = (1/m)*(z-y)
4.      da = np.dot(X.T, dz)
5.      db = np.sum(dz)
6.
7.      return da, db
```

The following script implements the function **update_parameters()**, which basically implements the gradient descent function explained in equations 7 and 8.

Script 8:

```
1.  def update_parameters(a, b, da, db, lr):
2.      a = a - lr * da
3.      b = b - lr * db
4.
5.      return a, b
```

Finally, the following script implements the regression function. The function accepts the input features, the target values, the number of epochs (the number of times you want to apply gradient descent), and the learning rate(lr). The learning rate defines how fast you want to learn. When the learning rate is too less, it results in slow learning, while a big learning rate may result in gradient overshooting.

Script 9:

```
1.  def linear_regression1(X, y, lr, epochs):
2.      error_list = []
3.      lenw = X.shape[1]
4.      a,b = define_parameters(lenw)
5.
```

```
6.         for i in range(epochs):
7.             z = predictions(a, b, X)
8.             cost = find_cost(z,y)
9.             error_list.append(cost)
10.            da, db = find_derivatives(X, y, z)
11.            a, b = update_parameters(a, b, da, db, lr)
12.            if i % 50 == 0 :
13.                print(cost)
14.
15.        return a, b, error_list
```

The following script calls the linear_regression1() method, which performs the gradient descent to reduce error. The cost or the error is printed after every 50 epochs.

Script 10:

```
1.   lr = 0.01
2.   epochs = 1000
3.   a, b, error_list = linear_regression1(X,y,lr,epochs)
```

Output:

```
5245.537901427559
2057.9130375799696
807.7254411472532
317.39503434318095
125.08257177225516
49.65495534839423
20.07093760954906
8.467484006886664
3.916342709698301
2.131269879574075
1.4311154909276216
1.1564945392812818
1.0487797705362227
1.006530583312928
0.989959046118921
0.9834591202843973
0.980909620200287
```

```
0.9799096143109023
0.9795173752216293
0.9793635243801215
```

The above output shows that the cost was initially 5245, which is reduced to 0.979 after 2,000 iterations. The following script plots the error.

Script 11:

```
1.    plt.plot(error_list)
```

Output:

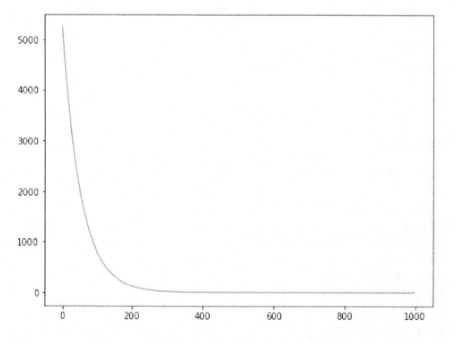

The output shows that we achieved the minimum error value around 200 epochs.

2.1.2. Multivariate Linear Regression

In multivariate linear regression, the number of input features is more than one. For instance, if you want to predict the price of the house (target label) based on the following input features: the number of bedrooms, the area in squares, distance from the city center, etc., the problem is categorized as multivariate linear regression since multiple input features are being used to predict the output.

The linear regression equation can be represented with a line. The multivariate linear regression slope is represented by a plane if there are two input features or a hyperplane in case of over two features.

The equation for the slope in case of multivariate linear equation is represented as:

$$Y = w1x1 + w2x2 + w3x3 + ...wnxn + b \quad ----------- (9)$$

In univariate linear regression, we had one weight a and one bias b. In the case of multivariate linear regression, the number of weights will be equal to the number of input features. In equation 9, the weights are represented by w1, w2, w3 .... Wn, where n is the number of total features. Here, the cost function would be:

$$J = \frac{1}{m} \sum_{i=1}^{m} ((w_1 x_{i1} + w_2 x_{i2} + \cdots w_n x_{in} + b) - y_i)^2$$

Since,

$$y^\wedge = (w_1 x_{i1} + w_2 x_{i2} + \cdots w_n x_{in} + b)$$

The derivative of the above cost function with respect to weight w1 is:

$$\frac{J\Delta}{J(w1)} = \frac{1}{m} \sum_{i=1}^{m} 2(y^\wedge - y)(x_{i1})$$

Similarly, for w2, the derivative will be:

$$\frac{J\Delta}{J(w2)} = \frac{1}{m}\sum_{i=1}^{m} 2(y^\wedge - y)(x_{i2})$$

And for wn:

$$\frac{J\Delta}{J(wn)} = \frac{1}{m}\sum_{i=1}^{m} 2(y^\wedge - y)(x_{in})$$

For b, the derivative will remain the same:

$$\frac{J\Delta}{J(b)} = \frac{1}{m}\sum_{i=1}^{m} 2(y^\wedge - y)$$

Again, you can remove 2 from all the derivatives since it is a constant.

Finally, here is the equation to apply gradient descent or to update the parameters:

$$wn = wn - lr * \frac{J\Delta}{J(wn)}$$

Equation 10: Gradient Descent Equation for Weight n

$$b = b - lr * \frac{J\Delta}{J(b)}$$

Equation 11: Gradient Descent Equation for Bias

Implementing Multivariate Linear Regression from Scratch in Python

Let's first create a dummy regression dataset with three features and one target variable. The features can be considered as the size, number of bedrooms, and distance from the city center, while the output variable can be considered as the price of the house.

Script 12:

```
1.  from sklearn.datasets import make_regression
2.  import matplotlib.pyplot as plt
3.  import numpy as np
4.
5.  X, y= make_regression(n_samples=100, n_features=3,
    noise=1.0, bias=50)
6.
7.  y = y.reshape(y.shape[0],1)
```

Let's check the shape of our dataset.

Script 13:

```
1.  print(X.shape)
2.  print(y.shape)
```

Output:

```
(100, 3)
(100, 1)
```

Script 14:

```
1.  def define_parameters(n_weights):
2.      a = np.random.randn( n_weights, 1)
3.      b = np.random.randn()
4.      return a, b
```

Script 15:

```
1.  def predictions(a, b , X):
2.      z = np.dot(X,a) + b
3.      return z
```

Script 16:

```
1.  def find_cost(z,y):
2.      m = y.shape[0]
3.      total_cost = (1/m) * np.sum(np.square(z - y))
4.      return total_cost
```

Script 17:

```
1.  def find_derivatives(X,y,z):
2.      m = y.shape[0]
3.      dz = (1/m)*(z-y)
4.      dw = np.dot(X.T, dz)
5.      db = np.sum(dz)
6.
7.      return dw, db
```

The following script implements the function **update_ parameters()**, which basically implements the gradient descent function.

Script 18:

```
1.  def update_parameters(a, b, da, db, lr):
2.      a = a - lr * da
3.      b = b - lr * db
4.
5.      return a, b
```

Finally, the following script implements the multivariate regression function.

Script 19:

```
1.   def linear_regressionm(X, y, lr, epochs):
2.       error_list = []
3.       lenw = X.shape[1]
4.       a,b = define_parameters(lenw)
5.
6.       for i in range(epochs):
7.           z = predictions(a, b, X)
8.           cost = find_cost(z,y)
9.           error_list.append(cost)
10.          da, db = find_derivatives(X, y, z)
11.          a, b = update_parameters(a, b, da, db, lr)
12.          if i % 50 == 0 :
13.              print(cost)
14.
15.      return error_list
```

The following script calls the **linear_regressionm()** method, which performs the gradient descent to reduce error. The cost or the error is printed after every 50 epochs.

Script 20:

```
1.   lr = 0.01
2.   epochs = 1000
3.   error_list = linear_regressionm(X,y,lr,epochs)
```

Output:

```
17461.950003132533
7260.946268081211
3055.4766569221965
1298.8832803638159
557.003170156412
240.763790365987
104.92221790851863
46.20062160956383
20.684353482630986
9.549659058573715
4.673923869777418
```

```
2.5328977556727743
1.5905870791890133
1.1750889440530479
0.9916065992015999
0.9104832693268997
0.8745809096388025
0.8586791757353913
0.8516315267106046
0.848506390322606
```

Script 21:

```
1.  plt.plot(error_list)
```

Output:

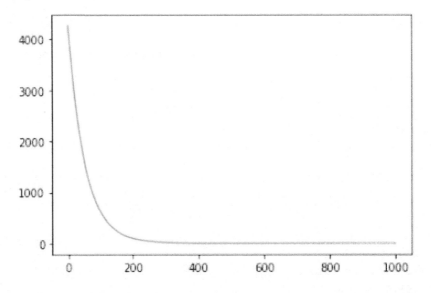

The output shows that we achieved the minimum error value around 200 epochs.

2.2. Logistic Regression

Logistic regression is a type of regression, where the output is either 0 or 1. Logistic regression can be used to perform binary classification tasks, such as whether or not a student will pass the exam or whether or not a certain bank account is fake, etc. It is extremely easy to convert a linear regression function to logistic regression. All you have to do is pass the output of the linear regression function as input to the Sigmoid function. The Sigmoid function quashes the input value between 0 and 1. If the value of the dot product of the weights and features is greater than 0.5, the Sigmoid function will quash it close to 1. If the value is less than 0.5, the Sigmoid function quashes it close to 0. The Sigmoid function looks like this:

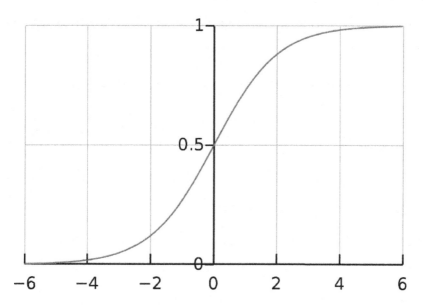

Now, while making predictions, you have to perform two tasks. First, you have to take the dot product of input features and weights. This is similar to linear regression and is shown below:

$$Z = w1x1 + w2x2 + \ldots\ldots wnxn + b$$

Next, the dot product is passed through the Sigmoid function, as shown below.

$$z = \frac{1}{1 + e^{-X.W}}$$

The derivative of the Sigmoid function is:

Sigmoid(x) * (1 - sigmoid(x).

Here, to calculate the derivative of W, you need to apply chain rule:

$$\frac{d\_cost}{d\_w} = \frac{d\_cost}{d\_pred} * \frac{d\_pred}{d\_z} * \frac{d\_z}{d\_w}$$

In the above equation, d_cost is the total cost with respect to predictions.

$$\frac{d\_cost}{d\_pred} = 2(predictions - observations)$$

Next, a prediction which is Sigmoid function is derived with respect to the dot product z.

$$\frac{d\_pred}{d\_z} = sigmoid(z) * (1 - sigmoid(z)$$

Finally, the dot product of z is taken with respect to the weight vector.

$$\frac{d\_z}{d\_w} = X.T$$

For b, the derivative is simply:

$$\frac{d\_cost}{d\_w} = \frac{d\_cost}{d\_pred} * \frac{d\_pred}{d\_z}$$

Implementing Logistic Regression from Scratch in Python

In this section, we will apply logistic regression from scratch in Python to predict if a banknote is authenticated or not.

The following script downloads the dataset.

Script 22:

```
1.  import pandas as pd
2.  import numpy as np
3.
4.  dataset = pd.read_csv("https://raw.githubusercontent.com/
    Kuntal-G/Machine-Learning/master/R-machine-learning/data/
    banknote-authentication.csv")
```

Script 23:

```
1.  dataset.head()
```

Output:

	variance	skew	curtosis	entropy	class
0	3.62160	8.6661	-2.8073	-0.44699	0
1	4.54590	8.1674	-2.4586	-1.46210	0
2	3.86600	-2.6383	1.9242	0.10645	0
3	3.45660	9.5228	-4.0112	-3.59440	0
4	0.32924	-4.4552	4.5718	-0.98880	0

The data can be divided into the feature and label sets by using the following script.

Script 24:

```
1.  X = dataset.drop(['class'], axis=1).values
2.
3.  y = dataset['class'].values
```

Next, we define a method that returns weights.

Script 25:

```
1.  def define_parameters(n_weights):
2.      w = np.random.randn( n_weights, 1)
3.      b = np.random.randn()
4.
5.      return w, b
```

The following two scripts define the Sigmoid function and the function that returns the derivative of the Sigmoid function.

Script 26:

```
1.  def sigmoid(x):
2.      return 1/(1+np.exp(-x))
```

Script 27:

```
1.  def sigmoid_der(x):
2.      return sigmoid(x)*(1-sigmoid(x))
```

Next, we make predictions using the following script.

Script 28:

```
1.  def predictions(w, b, X):
2.      XW = np.dot(X,w) + b
3.      z = sigmoid(XW)
4.      return z
```

The cost is calculated using script 29.

Script 29:

```
1.  def find_cost(z,y):
2.      m = y.shape[0]
3.      total_cost = (1/m) * np.sum(np.square(z - y))
4.      return total_cost
```

The following script finds the derivative of the cost function with respect to weights and bias.

Script 30:

```
1.   def find_derivatives(X,y,z):
2.       m = y.shape[0]
3.       dcost_dpred = (1/m)*(z-y)
4.       dpred_dz = sigmoid_der(z)
5.       z_delta = dcost_dpred * dpred_dz
6.       dz_dw = X.T
7.       dw = np.dot( dz_dw , z_delta)
8.       db = np.sum(z_delta)
9.
10.      return dw, db
```

The following function applies gradient descent and updates weights.

Script 31:

```
1.   def update_weights(w,b,dw,db,lr):
2.       w = w - lr * dw
3.       b = b - lr * db
4.
5.       return w, b
```

Finally, the following scripts define the parameters and find the derivatives.

Script 32:

```
1.  def multi_logistic_regression(X, y, lr, epochs):
2.      error_list = []
3.      lenw = X.shape[1]
4.      w,b = define_parameters(lenw)
5.      for i in range(epochs):
6.          z = predictions(w, b, X)
7.          cost = find_cost(z, y)
8.          error_list.append(cost)
9.          dw, db = find_derivatives (X,y,z)
10.         w, b = update_weights(w, b, dw, db,  lr )
11.         if i % 50 == 0 :
12.             print(cost)
13.
14.
15.     return w, b, error_list
```

Script 33:

```
1.  lr = 0.05
2.  epochs = 2000
3.  w, b, error_list = multi_logistic_
    regression(X,y,lr,epochs)
```

Output:

```
0.5914464164844608
0.23501171678589697
0.16047066512276695
0.12764567820457426
0.10738836050004111
0.09296245321485669
0.08186579463576191
0.07299211908622301
0.06578114358499872
0.05988373318642627
0.05503233600626867
0.05100693904544516
```

```
0.04762955737485885
0.04476063559314789
0.042293060350355389
0.0401453770327655
0.03825566874984804
0.036576624658974474
0.03507178548883319
0.033712762529804485
```

Script 34:

```
1.  plt.plot(error_list)
```

Output:

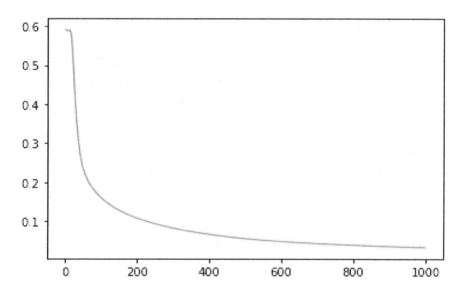

Let's finally check the accuracy of our logistic regression algorithm for authenticating banknote:

Script 35:

```
1.  z = predictions(w, b, X)
2.
3.  y_pred = []
4.  for i in z:
5.      if i > 5.0:
6.          y_pred.append(1)
7.      else:
8.          y_pred.append(0)
9.
10. y_true = sum(y.tolist() , [])
11.
12. correct = 0
13. for i in y_true :
14.     if y[i] == y_pred[i]:
15.         correct = correct + 1
16.
17. print("Accuracy: " + str(correct/len(y_true) * 100))
```

Output:

```
100.00
```

Our algorithm is 100 percent correct. Woohoo!

Exercise 2.1

Question 1

Which function is used at the last step to find the total error in case of logistic regression:

1. Mean Absolute Error
2. Sigmoid Function
3. Mean Squared Error
4. None of the above

Question 2

The number of weights + bias should be:

1. Equal to the number of input features in the data
2. More than the number of input features
3. Less than the number of input features
4. One more than the number of input features

Question 3

The purpose of gradient descent is to:

1. Minimize weights
2. Minimize bias
3. Maximize cost
4. Minimize cost

Exercise 2.2

Using the following dataset, apply logistic regression function to classify diabetic and non-diabetic patients. Print the accuracy as well. You can take help from section 2.2. in chapter 2.

```
1.  import pandas as pd
2.  import numpy as np
3.
4.  dataset = pd.read_csv("https://raw.githubusercontent.
    com/npradaschnor/Pima-Indians-Diabetes-Dataset/master/
    diabetes.csv")
5.  dataset.head()
```

3

Neural Networks from Scratch in Python

In the previous chapter, you understood how to implement linear and logistic regression algorithms from scratch in Python. In this chapter, you will learn how to implement neural networks from scratch in Python.

3.1. The Problem with Logistic/ Linear Regression

The main problem with the logistic and linear regression is that they cannot be used to learn non-linear boundaries. Logistic/ linear regression gives you a straight line and can only be used to predict or classify linear data. Most of the real-world problems are non-linear in nature, such as the one shown in the following figure:

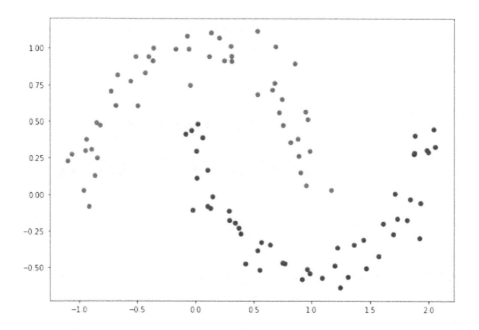

In the figure above, you cannot draw a straight line to differentiate the red points from blue points. Hence, logistic regression cannot be used to solve the above problem. In order to resolve this problem, you need non-linear boundaries. And neural network gives you exactly that. In the next sections, you will understand how to implement neural networks with a single output, and then you will understand how to implement neural networks with multiple outputs.

3.2. Neural Network with One Output

In this section, you will implement a neural network with a single output from scratch. You will be learning how to find a non-linear boundary to separate two classes. Let's define our dataset:

Script 1 :

```
1.  from sklearn import datasets
2.  import numpy as np
3.  import matplotlib.pyplot as plt
4.  %matplotlib inline
5.
6.  np.random.seed(0)
7.  X, y = datasets.make_moons(100, noise=0.10)
8.  x1 = X[:,0]
9.  x2 = X[:,1]
10.
11. plt.figure(figsize=(10,7))
12. plt.scatter(x1, x2, c= y, cmap=plt.cm.coolwarm)
```

Output:

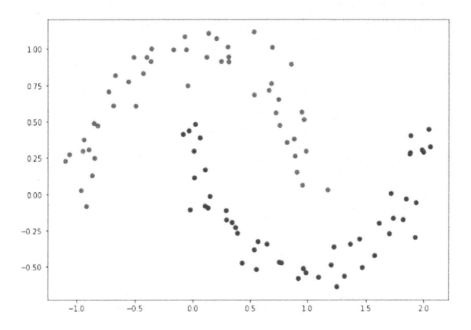

Our dataset has 100 records with two features and one output. You will need to reshape the output so that it has the same structure as the input features:

Script 2 :

```
1.  y = y.reshape(y.shape[0],1)
```

We can now check the shape of our input features and output labels:

Script 3 :

```
1.  print(X.shape)
2.  print(y.shape)
```

Output:

```
(100, 2)
(100, 1)
```

Before we move forward, let's define the structure of our neural network. Our neural network will look like this:

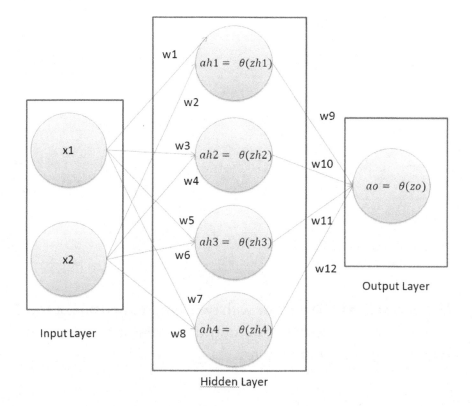

In a neural network, we have an input layer, one or multiple hidden layers, and an output layer. In our neural network, we have two nodes in the input layer (since there are two features in the input), one hidden layer with four nodes, and one output layer with one node since we are doing binary classification. The number of hidden layers and the number of neurons per hidden layer depend upon you.

In the above neural network, the x1 and x2 are the input features, and the ao is the output of the network. Here, the only thing we can control is the weights w1, w2, w3, ... w12. The idea is to find the values of weights for which the difference between the predicted output ao in this case and the actual output (labels).

A neural network works in two steps:

1. Feed Forward
2. Back Propagation

I will explain both these steps in the context of our neural network.

3.2.1. Feed Forward

In the feed forward step, the final output of a neural network is created. Let's try to find the final output of our neural network.

In our neural network, we will first find the value of zh1, which can be calculated as follows:

$$zh1 = x1w1 + x2w2 + b \text{ ---------- (1)}$$

Using zh1, we can find the value of ah1, which is:

$$ah1 = sigmoid(zh1) \text{ ---------- (2)}$$

In the same way, you find the values of ah2, ah3, and ah4.

To find the value of zo, you can use the following formula:

zo = ah1w9 + ah2w10 + ah3w11 + ah4w12 --------- (3)

Finally, to find the output of the neural network ao:

ao = sigmoid(zo) ---------- (4)

3.2.2. Backpropagation

The purpose of backpropagation is to minimize the overall loss by finding the optimum values of weights. The loss function used in this section is the mean squared error which is in our case represented as:

$$ J = \frac{1}{m} \sum_{i=1}^{m} (ao_i - y_i)^2 $$

Here, ao is the predicted output from our neural network, and y is the actual output.

Our weights are divided into two parts. We have weights that connect input features to the hidden layer and the hidden layer to the output node. We call the weights that connect the input to the hidden layer collectively as wh (w1, w2, w3 ...... w8), and the weights connecting the hidden layer to the output as wo (w9, w10, w11, w12).

The backpropagation will consist of two phases. In the first phase, we will find dcost_dwo (which refers to the derivative of the total cost) with respect to wo (weights in the output layer). By the chain rule, dcost_dwo can be represented as the product of dcost_dao * dao_dzo * dzo_dwo. (d here refers to derivative.) Mathematically:

dcost_dwo = dcost_dao * dao_dzo * dzo_dwo ------ (5)

dcost_dao = 1/m (ao – y) ------- (6)

dao_dzo = sigmoid(zo) * (1 – sigmoid(zo)) ------- (7)

dzo_dwo = ah.T ------ 8

In the same way, you find the derivative of cost with respect to bias in the output layer, i.e., dcost_dbo, which is given as:

dcost_dbo = dcost_dao * dao_dzo

Putting equations 6, 7, and 8 in equation 5, we can get the derivative of cost with respect to the output weights.

The next step is to find the derivative of cost with respect to hidden layer weights *wh* and bias *bh*. Let's first find the derivative of cost with respect to hidden layer weights:

dcost_dwh =dcost_dah * dah_dzh * dzh_dwh ..... (9)

dcost_dah= dcost_dao * dao_dzo * dzo_dah .... (10)

The values of dcost_dao and dao_dzo can be calculated from equations 6 and 7, respectively. The value of dzo_dah is given as:

dzo_dah = wo.T ...... (11)

Putting the values of equations 6, 7, and 11 in equation 11, you can get the value of equation10.

Next, let's find the value of dah_dzh:

dah_dzh = sigmoid(zh)*(1-sigmoid(zh) ..... (12)

and,

dzh_dwh = X.T (13)

Using equations 10, 12, and 13 in equation 9, you can find the value of dcost_dwh.

3.2.3. Implementation in Python

In this section, you will implement the neural network that we saw earlier, from scratch in Python.

Let's define a function that defines parameters:

Script 4 :

```
1.  def define_parameters(weights):
2.      weight_list = []
3.      bias_list = []
4.      for i in range(len(weights) - 1):
5.
6.          w = np.random.randn(weights[i], weights[i+1])
7.          b = np.random.randn()
8.
9.          weight_list.append(w)
10.         bias_list.append(b)
11.
12.     return weight_list, bias_list
```

Since now, we have multiple sets of weights, the defined parameters function will return a list of weights connecting the input and hidden layer and the hidden and output layer.

Next, we define the Sigmoid function and its derivative:

Script 5 :

```
1.  def sigmoid(x):
2.      return 1/(1+np.exp(-x))
```

Script 6 :

```
1.  def sigmoid_der(x):
2.      return sigmoid(x)*(1-sigmoid(x))
```

The feed forward part of the algorithm is implemented by the **prediction()** method as shown below:

Script 7 :

```
1.  def predictions(w, b, X):
2.      zh = np.dot(X,w[0]) + b[0]
3.      ah = sigmoid(zh)
4.
5.      zo = np.dot(ah, w[1]) + b[1]
6.      ao = sigmoid(zo)
7.      return ao
```

The following script defines the cost function:

Script 8 :

```
1.  def find_cost(ao,y):
2.      m = y.shape[0]
3.      total_cost = (1/m) * np.sum(np.square(ao - y))
4.      return total_cost
```

Finally, to implement the backpropagation, we create a **derivatives()** function as follows:

Script 9 :

```
1.  def find_derivatives(w, b, X):
2.
3.      zh = np.dot(X,w[0]) + b[0]
4.      ah = sigmoid(zh)
5.
6.      zo = np.dot(ah, w[1]) + b[1]
7.      ao = sigmoid(zo)
8.
9.      # Backpropagation phase 1
10.     m = y.shape[0]
11.     dcost_dao = (1/m)*(ao-y)
12.     dao_dzo = sigmoid_der(zo)
13.     dzo_dwo = ah.T
14.
15.     dwo =  np.dot(dzo_dwo, dcost_dao * dao_dzo)
16.     dbo = np.sum(dcost_dao * dao_dzo)
17.
```

```
18.      # Backpropagation phase 2
19.
20.      # dcost_wh = dcost_dah * dah_dzh * dzh_dwh
21.      # dcost_dah = dcost_dzo * dzo_dah
22.
23.      dcost_dzo = dcost_dao * dao_dzo
24.      dzo_dah = w[1].T
25.
26.      dcost_dah = np.dot(dcost_dzo , dzo_dah)
27.
28.      dah_dzh = sigmoid_der(zh)
29.      dzh_dwh = X.T
30.      dwh = np.dot(dzh_dwh, dah_dzh * dcost_dah)
31.      dbh = np.sum(dah_dzh * dcost_dah)
32.
33.      return dwh, dbh, dwo, dbo
```

And to update weights by subtracting the gradient, we define the **update_weights()** function.

Script 10 :

```
1.   def update_weights(w,b,dwh, dbh, dwo, dbo, lr):
2.       w[0] = w[0] - lr * dwh
3.       w[1] = w[1] - lr * dwo
4.
5.       b[0] = b[0] - lr * dbh
6.       b[1] = b[1] - lr * dbo
7.
8.       return w, b
```

Here is the **my_neural_network** class, which is used to train the neural network by implementing the feedforward and backward propagation steps.

Script 11 :

```
1.  def my_neural_network(X, y, lr, epochs):
2.      error_list = []
3.      input_len = X.shape[1]
4.      output_len = y.shape[1]
5.      w,b = define_parameters([input_len, 4, output_len])
6.
7.      for i in range(epochs):
8.          ao = predictions(w, b, X)
9.          cost = find_cost(ao, y)
10.         error_list.append(cost)
11.         dwh, dbh, dwo, dbo = find_derivatives (w, b, X)
12.         w, b = update_weights(w, b, dwh, dbh, dwo, dbo,
    lr )
13.         if i % 50 == 0 :
14.             print(cost)
15.
16.     return w, b, error_list
```

Let's train our neural network now to see the error reducing:

Script 12:

```
1.  lr = 0.5
2.  epochs = 2000
3.  w, b, error_list = my_neural_network(X,y,lr,epochs)
```

Output:

```
0.1980211046202944
0.14097327813016874
0.1199356196746553
0.10996149384567079
0.1046354602995857
0.10125014770369335
0.09877988582294377
0.09681954900387213
0.09519153134310644
0.09380667924462933
0.09261322597192048
0.09157694024355723
0.0906728783113126
```

```
0.0898816633148205
0.08918762513676567
0.08857775866745798
0.0880410781190082
0.08756818639880107
0.08715097414153263
0.08678240229725143
0.08645634002244419
0.08616743928189777
0.08591103380363199
0.08568305442008338
0.0854799559120146
0.08529865252129894
0.08513646055443663
0.08499104719247362
0.08486038495701591
0.08474271141085092
0.08463649370001301
0.08454039753494193
0.08445326019470517
0.08437406713419247
0.08430193178325884
0.08423607814745766
0.0841758258488823
0.08412057727921075
0.08406980657236514
0.08402305013908634
```

In the output, it is evident that the error is reducing. Let's plot the error value on a plot:

Script 13:

```
1.    plt.plot(error_list)
```

Output:

```
[<matplotlib.lines.Line2D at 0x7f8e094b94e0>]
```

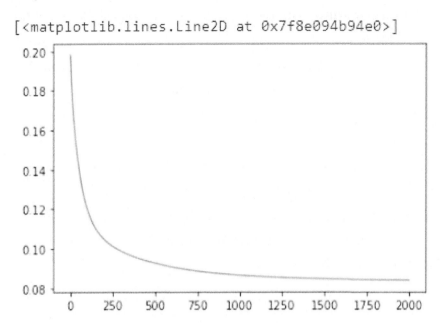

You can see that the error is decreased with each epoch.

The process of implementing a neural network with one output from scratch in Python is very similar to logistic regression. However, in this case, we had to update two sets of weights, one in the hidden layer and one in the output layer.

3.3. Neural Network with Multiple Outputs

In the previous section, you did a binary classification where you predicted whether a point is red or blue. In most real-world applications, you have to classify between more than two objects. For instance, you might be given an image, and you have to guess the single digit in the image. In that case, the number of possible outputs will be 0-9 = 10. The type of problems where you have more than two possible outputs is called multiclass classification problems.

To implement multiclass classification problems, you have to make three changes in the neural network with a single output. The changes are as follows:

1. In the output layer, the number of nodes should be equal to the number of possible outputs.

2. The Softmaxactivation function should be used in the final output layer.

3. To reduce the cost, a negative log likelihood function should be used as the loss function.

We will not cover in depth the Softmax and negative log likelihood functions in this chapter. Here is a very good blog to understand the Softmax function:

https://medium.com/data-science-bootcamp/understand-the-softmax-function-in-minutes-f3a59641e86d

And here is a very good blog to understand the negative log likelihood:

https://medium.com/deeplearningmadeeasy/negative-log-likelihood-6bd79b55d8b6

In this chapter, we will develop a neural network with three possible outputs. Let's first create the dataset for that:

Execute the following script:

Script 14 :

```
1.   import numpy as np
2.   import matplotlib.pyplot as plt
3.
4.   np.random.seed(42)
5.
6.   cat1 = np.random.randn(800, 2) + np.array([0, -3])
7.   cat2 = np.random.randn(800, 2) + np.array([3, 3])
8.   cat3 = np.random.randn(800, 2) + np.array([-3, 3])
9.
10.  X = np.vstack([cat1, cat2, cat3])
11.
12.  labels = np.array([0]*800 + [1]*800 + [2]*800)
13.
14.  y = np.zeros((2400, 3))
15.
16.  for i in range(2400):
17.      y[i, labels[i]] = 1
```

Let's check the shape of our dataset:

Script 15 :

```
1.   print(X.shape)
2.   print(y.shape)
```

Output:

```
(2400, 2)
(2400, 3)
```

The output shows that we have 2,400 records in our dataset. The input contains two features, and the output contains three possible labels. (Each row in the output contains three columns, one column for each label.)

Next, we will plot our dataset to see the three classes:

Script 16 :

```
1.    x1 = X[:,0]
2.    x2 = X[:,1]
3.
4.    plt.figure(figsize=(10,7))
5.    plt.scatter(x1, x2, c= y, cmap=plt.cm.coolwarm)
```

Output:

`<matplotlib.collections.PathCollection at 0x7f289391fe48>`

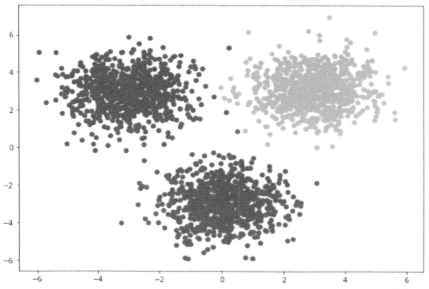

From the output, it is evident that our dataset records can either be represented by a red, green, or blue dot, which means that we have three possible labels in the output. Also, these labels cannot be separated by a straight line. Hence, we will be using a neural network with multiple outputs. The architecture of the neural network will look like this:

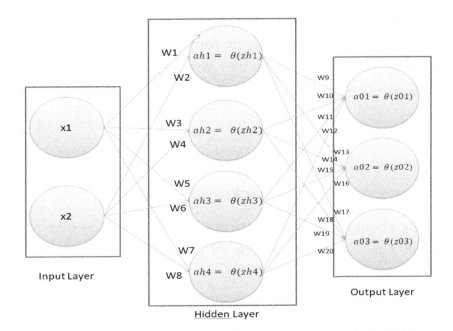

You can see that this neural network is very similar to the neural network that we saw earlier. Except now, we have three nodes in the output, and hence, more number of weights in the output layer. Let's see the feedforward process for the above neural network:

3.1.1. Feed Forward

Let's briefly review the feed forward step for a neural network with multiple steps. To

$$zh1 = x1w1 + x2w2 + b \text{ ---------- (14)}$$

Using zh1, we can find the value of ah1, which is:

$$ah1 = sigmoid(zh1) \text{ ---------- (15)}$$

In the same way, you find the values of ah2, ah3, and ah4.

To find the value of zo, you can use the following formula:

$$zo1 = ah1w9 + ah2w10 + ah3w11 + ah4w12 \text{ --------- (16)}$$

Similarly, you can calculate the values for zo2 and zo3. The output will be a vector of the form [3,1]. This vector will be passed to the Softmax function, which also returns a vector of [3,1], which will be our final output ao.

Hence,

$$ao = softmax(vector \ [zo]) \ \text{----------} \ (17)$$

3.1.2. Backpropagation

In the backpropagation step, you have to find the derivative of the cost function with respect to the weights in a different layer. Let's first find dcost_dwo:

$$dcost\_dwo = dcost\_dzo * dzo\_dwo \ \text{------} \ (18)$$

The derivative of the negative log likelihood function with respect to the values in the zo vector is:

$$dcost\_dzo = ao - y \ \text{--------} \ (19)$$

In equation 19, y is the actual output. Similarly, we can find dzo_dwo as follows:

$$dzo\_dwo = ah.T \ \text{-----} \ (20)$$

Putting equations 19 and 20 in equation 18, you can get the derivate of cost with respect to the weights in the output layer, i.e., wo.

Similarly, dcost_dbo is equal to:

$$dcost\_dbo = dcost\_dzo \ \text{----} \ (21)$$

Next, we need to find the dcost_dwh which is given as:

$$dcost\_dwh = dcost\_dah* \ dah\_dzh * dzh\_dwh \ \text{------} \ (22)$$

$$dcost\_dah = dcost\_dzo * dzo\_dah \ \text{----} \ (23)$$

$$dzo\_dah = wo.T \ \text{--------} \ (24)$$

Putting the value of equations 19 and 24 in equation 23, you can get the value of dcost_dah.

Next,

$$dah\_dzh = sigmoid(zh) * (1- sigmoid(zh)) \text{ ------- (25)}$$

$$dzh\_dwh = ah.T \text{ ------------ (26)}$$

Putting the value of equations 23, 25, and 26 in equation 22, you can find the value of dost_dwh.

3.3.3. Implementation in Python

Let's now see the Python implementation of a neural network with multiple outputs:

Script 17:

```
1.   import numpy as np
2.   import matplotlib.pyplot as plt
3.
4.   np.random.seed(42)
5.
6.   cat1 = np.random.randn(800, 2) + np.array([0, -3])
7.   cat2 = np.random.randn(800, 2) + np.array([3, 3])
8.   cat3 = np.random.randn(800, 2) + np.array([-3, 3])
9.
10.
11.  X = np.vstack([cat1, cat2, cat3])
12.
13.  labels = np.array([0]*800 + [1]*800 + [2]*800)
14.
15.  y = np.zeros((2400, 3))
16.
17.  for i in range(2400):
18.      y[i, labels[i]] = 1
19.  print(X.shape)
20.  print(y.shape)
21.  x1 = X[:,0]
```

```python
22. x2 = X[:,1]
23.
24. plt.figure(figsize=(10,7))
25. plt.scatter(x1, x2, c= y, cmap=plt.cm.coolwarm)
26. def define_parameters(weights):
27.     weight_list = []
28.     bias_list = []
29.     for i in range(len(weights) - 1):
30.
31.         w = np.random.randn(weights[i], weights[i+1])
32.         b = np.random.randn()
33.
34.         weight_list.append(w)
35.         bias_list.append(b)
36.
37.     return weight_list, bias_list
38. def softmax(X):
39.     expX = np.exp(X)
40.     return expX / expX.sum(axis=1, keepdims=True)
41. def sigmoid(x):
42.     return 1/(1+np.exp(-x))
43. def sigmoid_der(x):
44.     return sigmoid(x)*(1-sigmoid(x))
45. def predictions(w, b, X):
46.     zh = np.dot(X,w[0]) + b[0]
47.     ah = sigmoid(zh)
48.
49.     zo = np.dot(ah, w[1]) + b[1]
50.     ao = softmax(zo)
51.     return ao
52.
53. def find_cost(ao,y):
54.
55.     total_cost = np.sum(-y * np.log(ao))
56.     return total_cost
57.
58. def find_derivatives(w, b, X):
59.
60.     zh = np.dot(X,w[0]) + b[0]
```

```
61.        ah = sigmoid(zh)
62.
63.        zo = np.dot(ah, w[1]) + b[1]
64.        ao = softmax(zo)
65.
66.        # Back propagation phase 1
67.
68.
69.        dcost_dzo = (ao-y)
70.        dzo_dwo = ah.T
71.
72.        dwo =  np.dot(dzo_dwo,  dcost_dzo)
73.        dbo = np.sum(dcost_dzo)
74.
75.        # Back propagation phase 2
76.
77.        # dcost_wh = dcost_dah * dah_dzh * dzh_dwh
78.        # dcost_dah = dcost_dzo * dzo_dah
79.
80.
81.        dzo_dah = w[1].T
82.
83.        dcost_dah = np.dot(dcost_dzo , dzo_dah)
84.
85.        dah_dzh = sigmoid_der(zh)
86.        dzh_dwh = X.T
87.        dwh = np.dot(dzh_dwh, dah_dzh * dcost_dah)
88.        dbh = np.sum(dah_dzh * dcost_dah)
89.
90.        return dwh, dbh, dwo, dbo
91. def update_weights(w,b,dwh, dbh, dwo, dbo, lr):
92.        w[0] = w[0] - lr * dwh
93.        w[1] = w[1] - lr * dwo
94.
95.        b[0] = b[0] - lr * dbh
96.        b[1] = b[1] - lr * dbo
97.
98.        return w, b
99. def my_multiout_neural_network(X, y, lr, epochs):
```

```
100.    error_list = []
101.    input_len = X.shape[1]
102.    output_len = y.shape[1]
103.    w,b = define_parameters([input_len, 4, output_len])
104.
105.    for i in range(epochs):
106.        ao = predictions(w, b, X)
107.        cost = find_cost(ao, y)
108.        error_list.append(cost)
109.        dwh, dbh, dwo, dbo = find_derivatives (w, b, X)
110.        w, b = update_weights(w, b, dwh, dbh, dwo, dbo,
    lr )
111.        if i % 50 == 0 :
112.            print(cost)
113.
114.    return w, b, error_list
115.
116.
117. lr = 0.0005
118. epochs = 1000
119. w, b, error_list = my_multiout_neural_
    network(X,y,lr,epochs)
```

Output:

```
4921.784443712775
115.05275654791413
60.7093977747567
43.422649664931626
34.88864651152795
29.785198170132094
26.38081266811703
23.942717399078127
22.107134982438154
20.67281284937415
19.519299319106253
18.570055076513714
17.774096074967886
```

```
17.09614091195548
16.51099321192574
16.000176100360964
15.549830828069574
15.149357906344129
14.790511529599819
14.466780088357714
```

The output shows that the error is decreasing. Let's plot the error against the epochs:

Script 18:

```
1.   plt.plot(error_list)
```

Output:

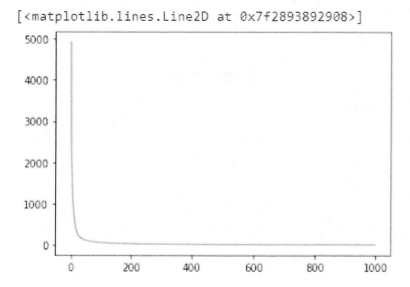

You can clearly see error decreasing quickly initially, and then very slowly.

Let's now try to make prediction on a single data point:

Script 19 :

```
1.  pred = predictions(w, b, X[900].reshape(1,2))
2.  print(np.argmax(pred))
3.  print(np.argmax(y[900]))
```

In the script above, we pick the data point at the 900th index and pass it to the predictions() method along with the weights and bias, and then we can find the index of the prediction and the actual output. If both indexes match, we can say that our prediction is true.

Output:

```
1
1
```

The output shows that the index of both the predicted and actual output is 1. Hence, our prediction is correct.

Exercise 3.1

Question 1:

In a neural network with three input features, one hidden layer of five nodes, and an output layer with three possible values, what will be the dimensions of weight that connects the input to the hidden layer? Remember, the dimensions of the input data is (m,3) where m are the number of records.

1. [5,3]
2. [3,5]
3. [4,5]
4. [5,4]

Question 2:

Which activation function do you use in the output layer in the case of multiclass classification problems:

1. Sigmoid
2. Negative log likelihood
3. Relu
4. Softmax

Question 3:

Neural networks with hidden layers are capable of finding:

1. Linear Boundaries
2. Non-linear Boundaries
3. All of the above
4. None of the Above

Exercise 3.2

Try to classify the following dataset with three classes by implementing a multiclass classification neural network from scratch in Python.

```
1.   import numpy as np
2.   import matplotlib.pyplot as plt
3.
4.   np.random.seed(42)
5.
6.   cat1 = np.random.randn(800, 2) + np.array([0, -2])
7.   cat2 = np.random.randn(800, 2) + np.array([2, 2])
8.   cat3 = np.random.randn(800, 2) + np.array([-3, -3])
9.
10.
```

```
11. X = np.vstack([cat1, cat2, cat3])
12.
13. labels = np.array([0]*800 + [1]*800 + [2]*800)
14.
15. y = np.zeros((2400, 3))
16.
17. for i in range(2400):
18.     y[i, labels[i]] = 1
19.
20.
21. x1 = X[:,0]
22. x2 = X[:,1]
23.
24. plt.figure(figsize=(10,7))
25. plt.scatter(x1, x2, c= y, cmap=plt.cm.coolwarm)
```

<matplotlib.collections.PathCollection at 0x7f288732e6d8>

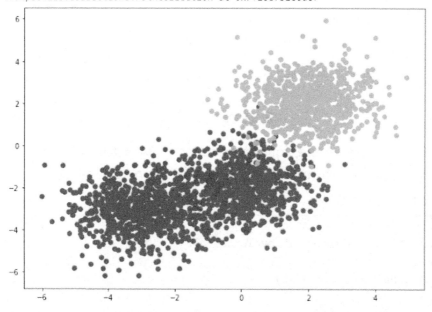

4

Introduction to TensorFlow and Keras

4.1. Introduction

In this chapter, you will be introduced to TensorFlow Keras API, using which you will be able to create Densely Connected Neural Networks for classification and regression tasks. We will be using TensorFlow 2.0 and Keras API to implement our script in this chapter. From TensorFlow 2.0, Google has officially adopted Keras as the main API to run TensorFlow scripts.

We know that supervised learning problems can be classified into two main sub-categories: classification and regression. In classification problems, you have to predict a predefined label for a data record, whereas for regression, you have to predict a particular value. Let's first see how to create a neural network for classification in TensorFlow 2.0.

4.2. Neural Network in TensorFlow for Classification (Binary Output)

Based on the output, the classification problems can be further divided into two types: Binary Classification and Multiclass Classification. In the binary classification problems, there can be only two possible outputs. For instance, predicting the face of a single coin toss can have one of the two possible values, i.e., heads or tails. In multiclass classification problems, there can be more than two possible outputs. For instance, time of the day, i.e., morning, afternoon, evening, or day of the week, or colors, etc.

In this section, you will understand how to perform classification with binary outputs. You will be predicting whether or not a banknote is genuine or not, based on certain features such as variance, skewness, curtosis, and entropy of several banknote images. Let's begin without ado.

The following script upgrades the existing TensorFlow version. I always recommend doing this.

Script 1:

```
1.   pip install --upgrade tensorflow
```

To check if you are actually running TensorFlow 2.0, execute the following command.

Script 2:

```
1.   import tensorflow as tf
2.   print(tf.__version__)
```

You should see 2.x.x in the output, as shown below:

Output:

```
2.1.0
```

Importing Required Libraries

Let's import the required libraries.

Script 3:

```
1.  import seaborn as sns
2.  import pandas as pd
3.  import numpy as np
4.
5.  from tensorflow.keras.layers import Dense, Dropout,
    Activation
6.  from tensorflow.keras.models import Model, Sequential
7.  from tensorflow.keras.optimizers import Adam
```

Importing the Dataset

The dataset we use here can be downloaded for free from the following GitHub resource. The dataset is also available in the *Resource* folder that accompanies this book.

Script 4:

```
1.  banknote_data = pd.read_csv("https://raw.
    githubusercontent.com/AbhiRoy96/Banknote-Authentication-
    UCI-Dataset/master/bank_notes.csv")
```

The following script plots the first five rows of the dataset.

Script 5:

```
1.  banknote_data.head()
```

Output:

	variance	skewness	curtosis	entropy	Target
0	3.62160	8.6661	-2.8073	-0.44699	0
1	4.54590	8.1674	-2.4586	-1.46210	0
2	3.86600	-2.6383	1.9242	0.10645	0
3	3.45660	9.5228	-4.0112	-3.59440	0
4	0.32924	-4.4552	4.5718	-0.98880	0

The output shows that our dataset contains five columns. Let's see the shape of our dataset.

Script 6:

```
1.    banknote_data.shape
```

The output shows that our dataset has 1,372 rows and 5 columns.

Output:

```
(1372, 5)
```

Let's plot a count plot to see the distribution of data with respect to the values in the class that we want to predict.

Script 7:

```
1.    sns.countplot(x='Target', data=banknote_data)
```

Output:

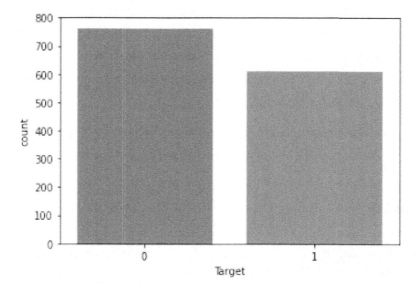

The output shows that the number of fake notes (represented by 1) is slightly less than the number of original banknotes.

The task is to predict the values for the *Target* column, based on the values in the first four columns. Let's divide our data into features and target labels.

Script 8:

```
1.  X = banknote_data.drop(['Target'], axis=1).values
2.  y = banknote_data[['Target']].values
3.
4.  print(X.shape)
5.  print(y.shape)
```

Output:

```
(1372, 4)
(1372, 1)
```

The variable X contains our feature set while the variable y contains target labels.

§ Dividing Data into Training and Test Sets

Deep learning models are normally trained on one set of data and are tested on another set. The dataset used to train a deep learning model is called a training set, and the dataset used to evaluate the performance of a trained deep learning model is called a test set.

We will divide the total data into an 80 percent training set and a 20 percent test set. The following script performs that task.

Script 9:

```
1.  from sklearn.model_selection import train_test_split
2.  X_train, X_test, y_train, y_test = train_test_split(X, y,
    test_size=0.20, random_state=42)
```

Before you train your deep learning model, it is always a good practice to scale your data. The following script applies standard scaling to training and test sets.

Script 10:

```
1.  from sklearn.preprocessing import StandardScaler
2.  sc = StandardScaler()
3.  X_train = sc.fit_transform(X_train)
4.  X_test = sc.transform(X_test)
```

§ Creating a Neural Network

To create a neural network, you can use the **Sequential** class from the **tensorflow.keras.models** module. To add layers to your model, you simply need to call the add method and pass your layer to it. To create a dense layer, you can use the **Dense** class.

The first parameter to the **Dense** class is the number of nodes in the dense layer, and the second parameter is the dimension of the input. The activation function can be defined by passing a string value to the activation attribute of the Dense class. It is important to mention that the input dimensions are only required to be passed to the first dense layer. The subsequent dense layers can calculate the input dimensions automatically from the number of nodes in the previous layers.

The following script defines a method `create_model`. The model takes two parameters: `learning_rate` and `dropout_rate`. Inside the model, we create an object of the `Sequential` class and add three dense layers to the model. The layers contain 12, 6, and 1 nodes, respectively. After each dense layer, we add a dropout layer with a dropout rate of 0.1.

Adding dropout after each layer avoids overfitting. After the model is created, compile it via the compile method. The compile method takes the loss function, the optimizer, and the metrics as parameters. Remember, for binary classification, the activation function in the final dense layer will be `sigmoid,` whereas the loss function in the compile method will be `binary_crossentropy`.

Script 11:

```
1.   def create_model(learning_rate, dropout_rate):
2.
3.       model = Sequential()
4.       model.add(Dense(12, input_dim=X_train.shape[1],
     activation='relu'))
5.       model.add(Dropout(dropout_rate))
6.       model.add(Dense(6,  activation='relu'))
7.       model.add(Dropout(dropout_rate))
8.       model.add(Dense(1, activation='sigmoid'))
9.
10.      adam = Adam(lr=learning_rate)
11.      model.compile(loss='binary_crossentropy',
     optimizer=adam, metrics=['accuracy'])
12.      return model
```

Next, we need to define the default dropout rate, learning rate batch size, and the number of epochs. The number of epochs refers to the number of times the whole dataset is used for training, and the batch size refers to the number of records after which the weights are updated.

```
1.   dropout_rate = 0.1
2.   epochs = 20
3.   batch_size = 4
4.   learn_rate = 0.001
```

The following script creates our model.

Script 12:

```
1.   model = create_model(learn_rate, dropout_rate)
```

You can see your model architecture via the **plot_model()** method of the **tensorflow.keras.utils** module.

Script 13:

```
1.  from tensorflow.keras.utils import plot_model
2.  plot_model(model, to_file='model_plot1.png', show_
    shapes=True, show_layer_names=True)
```

Output:

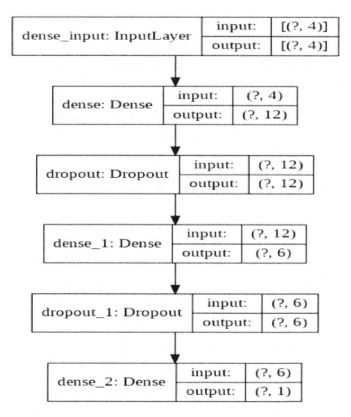

It is clearly evident from the above output that the input layer contains 4 nodes, the input to the first dense layers is 4 while the output is 12. Similarly, the input to the second dense layer is 12, while the output is 6. Finally, in the last dense layer, the input is 6 nodes, while the output is 1 since we are making a binary classification. Also, you can see a dropout layer after each dense layer.

To train the model, you need to call the fit method on the model object. The fit method takes the training features and targets as parameters, along with the batch size, the number of epochs, and the validation split. The validation split refers to the split in the training data during training.

Script 14:

```
1.  model_history = model.fit(X_train, y_train, batch_
    size=batch_size, epochs=epochs, validation_split=0.2,
    verbose=1)
```

The result from the last five epochs is shown below:

Output:

```
Epoch 15/20
877/877 [==============================] - 1s 1ms/sample - loss: 0.0230 - accuracy: 0.9943 - val_loss: 0.0067 - val_accuracy: 1.0000
Epoch 16/20
877/877 [==============================] - 1s 1ms/sample - loss: 0.0209 - accuracy: 0.9954 - val_loss: 0.0051 - val_accuracy: 1.0000
Epoch 17/20
877/877 [==============================] - 1s 1ms/sample - loss: 0.0204 - accuracy: 0.9977 - val_loss: 0.0040 - val_accuracy: 1.0000
Epoch 18/20
877/877 [==============================] - 1s 1ms/sample - loss: 0.0136 - accuracy: 0.9977 - val_loss: 0.0040 - val_accuracy: 1.0000
Epoch 19/20
877/877 [==============================] - 1s 1ms/sample - loss: 0.0234 - accuracy: 0.9954 - val_loss: 0.0047 - val_accuracy: 1.0000
Epoch 20/20
877/877 [==============================] - 1s 1ms/sample - loss: 0.0176 - accuracy: 0.9943 - val_loss: 0.0030 - val_accuracy: 1.0000
```

Our neural network is now trained. The "val_accuracy" of 1.0 in the last epoch shows that on the training set, our neural network is making predictions with 100 percent accuracy.

§ Evaluating the Neural Network Performance

We can now evaluate its performance by making predictions on the test set. To make predictions on the test set, pass the set to the evaluate() method of the model, as shown below:

Script 15:

```
1.  accuracies = model.evaluate(X_test, y_test, verbose=1)
2.
3.  print("Test Score:", accuracies[0])
4.  print("Test Accuracy:", accuracies[1])
```

Output:

```
275/275 [==============================] - 0s 374us/sample -
loss: 0.0040 - accuracy: 1.0000
Test Score: 0.003973540013286531
Test Accuracy: 1.0
```

The output shows an accuracy of 100 percent on the test set. The loss value of 0.00397 is shown. Remember, lower the loss, higher the accuracy.

Let's now plot the accuracy on the training and test set to see if our model is overfitting or not.

Script 16:

```
1.  import matplotlib.pyplot as plt
2.
3.  plt.plot(model_history.history['accuracy'], label =
    'accuracy')
4.  plt.plot(model_history.history['val_accuracy'], label =
    'val_accuracy')
5.  plt.legend(['train','test'], loc='lower left')
```

Output:

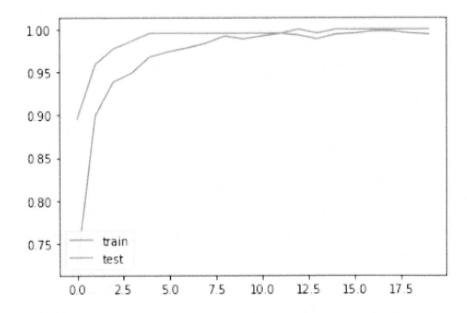

The above curve meets near 1, and then becomes stable which shows that our model is not overfitting.

Similarly, the loss values for test and training sets can be printed as follows:

Script 17:

```
1.  plt.plot(model_history.history['loss'], label = 'loss')
2.  plt.plot(model_history.history['val_loss'], label = 'val_
    loss')
3.  plt.legend(['train','test'], loc='upper left')
```

Output:

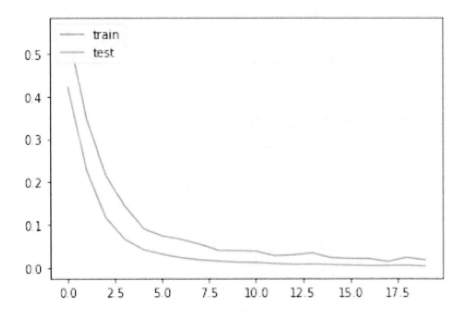

And this is it. You have successfully trained a neural network for classifying binary outputs. In the next section, you will look in depth at how to create a densely connected neural network for multiclass classification.

4.3. Neural Network in TensorFlow for Classification (Multiclass Output)

In a multiclass classification, the number of target labels is greater than 2. The process of binary and multiclass classification using a neural network in TensorFlow Keras is quite similar. You have to make three changes in the binary classification code:

1. Change the number of nodes in the final dense layer to the number of target labels in the output.

2. Change the activation function in the final dense layer from **sigmoid** to **softmax**.

3. Change the loss function in the compile method of the model from **binary_crossentropy** to **categorical_crossentropy**.

§ Importing the Required Libraries

The following script imports the required libraries.

Script 18:

```
1.  import seaborn as sns
2.  import pandas as pd
3.  import numpy as np
4.
5.  from tensorflow.keras.layers import Dense, Dropout,
    Activation
6.  from tensorflow.keras.models import Model, Sequential
7.  from tensorflow.keras.optimizers import Adam
```

Importing the Dataset

The following script imports the dataset. The dataset comes prebuilt with the **Seaborn** library. Therefore, you do not have to download it.

Script 19:

```
1.  iris_data = sns.load_dataset('iris')
2.  iris_data.head()
```

Output:

	sepal_length	sepal_width	petal_length	petal_width	species
0	5.1	3.5	1.4	0.2	setosa
1	4.9	3.0	1.4	0.2	setosa
2	4.7	3.2	1.3	0.2	setosa
3	4.6	3.1	1.5	0.2	setosa
4	5.0	3.6	1.4	0.2	setosa

Our dataset contains different attributes of the iris plant along with the species of the plant. Using the first four attributes, we have to predict the species of the plant. There can be three possible outputs: setosa, versicolor, and virginica. Since the number of target labels is greater than two, this problem is treated as a multiclass classification problem.

Let's divide the data into features and labels set. It is important to mention that TensorFlow neural networks work with numbers. Whenever we encounter text data, we have to convert it into numbers. Our output labels are in the form of text. We can convert the output into one-hot encoded numbers using **pd.get_dummies()** method, as shown below:

Script 20:

```
1.  X = iris_data.drop(['species'], axis=1)
2.  y = pd.get_dummies(iris_data.species, prefix='output')
3.  X.head()
```

The output shows the feature set:

Output:

	sepal_length	sepal_width	petal_length	petal_width
0	5.1	3.5	1.4	0.2
1	4.9	3.0	1.4	0.2
2	4.7	3.2	1.3	0.2
3	4.6	3.1	1.5	0.2
4	5.0	3.6	1.4	0.2

The following script prints the one-hot encoded output target labels.

Script 21:

```
1.  y.head()
```

The dimensions of the output should be R X O where R is the number of records, and O is the number of possible target variables, which in our case is 3.

Output:

	output_setosa	output_versicolor	output_virginica
0	1	0	0
1	1	0	0
2	1	0	0
3	1	0	0
4	1	0	0

The following script converts our features and labels set into numpy arrays since TensorFlow expects input data in the form of numpy arrays.

Script 22:

```
1.  X = X.values
2.  y = y.values
```

Dividing the Data into Training and Test Sets

The script below divides the data into training and test sets and then performs standard scaling on both the sets.

Script 23:

```
1.  from sklearn.model_selection import train_test_split
2.  X_train, X_test, y_train, y_test = train_test_split(X, y,
    test_size=0.20, random_state=42)
```

Script 24:

```
1.  from sklearn.preprocessing import StandardScaler
2.  sc = StandardScaler()
3.  X_train = sc.fit_transform(X_train)
4.  X_test = sc.transform(X_test)
```

§ Creating a Neural Network Model

As I said earlier, the neural network will be similar to the one we created for binary classification. However, in this case, the activation function in the final dense layer will be **softmax**. The number of nodes in the final dense layer will be equal to the number of target labels. And the loss function in the compile method will be **categorical_crossentropy**. Execute the following script to define the method that creates our neural network.

Script 25:

```
1.  def create_model_multiple_outs(learning_rate, dropout_
    rate):
2.
3.      model = Sequential()
4.      model.add(Dense(12, input_dim=X_train.shape[1],
    activation='relu'))
5.      model.add(Dropout(dropout_rate))
6.      model.add(Dense(6, activation='relu'))
7.      model.add(Dropout(dropout_rate))
8.      model.add(Dense(y_train.shape[1],
    activation='softmax'))
9.
10.     adam = Adam(lr=learning_rate)
11.     model.compile(loss='categorical_crossentropy',
    optimizer=adam, metrics=['accuracy'])
12.     return model
```

The following script defines the dropout, learning rate, epochs, and batch size. You can tweek these values to see if you can get better results.

Script 26:

```
1.  dropout_rate = 0.1
2.  epochs = 50
3.  batch_size = 1
4.  learn_rate = 0.001
```

The following script creates the actual model by calling the **model_multiple_outs()** that we created in Script 25. The script also prints the structure of the neural network model as shown by the output.

Script 27:

```
1.  model = create_model_multiple_outs(learn_rate, dropout_
    rate)
2.  from tensorflow.keras.utils import plot_model
3.  plot_model(model, to_file='model_plot1.png', show_
    shapes=True, show_layer_names=True)
```

Output:

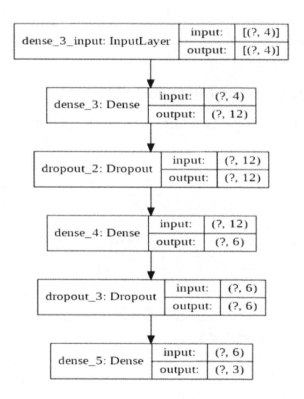

The following script trains the model by calling the **fit** method.

Script 28:

```
1.  model_history = model.fit(X_train, y_train, batch_
    size=batch_size, epochs=epochs, validation_split=0.2,
    verbose=1)
```

Output:

```
Epoch 45/50
96/96 [==============================] - 0s 4ms/sample - loss: 0.1804 - accuracy: 0.9375 - val_loss: 0.1126 - val_accuracy: 0.9583
Epoch 46/50
96/96 [==============================] - 0s 4ms/sample - loss: 0.1591 - accuracy: 0.9479 - val_loss: 0.0994 - val_accuracy: 0.9583
Epoch 47/50
96/96 [==============================] - 0s 4ms/sample - loss: 0.1393 - accuracy: 0.9583 - val_loss: 0.1094 - val_accuracy: 0.9583
Epoch 48/50
96/96 [==============================] - 0s 4ms/sample - loss: 0.1692 - accuracy: 0.9375 - val_loss: 0.1017 - val_accuracy: 0.9583
Epoch 49/50
96/96 [==============================] - 0s 4ms/sample - loss: 0.1428 - accuracy: 0.9375 - val_loss: 0.1001 - val_accuracy: 0.9583
Epoch 50/50
96/96 [==============================] - 0s 4ms/sample - loss: 0.1248 - accuracy: 0.9792 - val_loss: 0.1081 - val_accuracy: 0.9583
```

The output shows the result from the last five epochs. The result shows that the final accuracy of 95.83 percent is achieved on the training set.

Evaluating the Neural Network Model

The following script evaluates the model performance on the test.

Script 29:

```
1.  accuracies = model.evaluate(X_test, y_test, verbose=1)
2.
3.  print("Test Score:", accuracies[0])
4.  print("Test Accuracy:", accuracies[1])
```

Output:

```
30/30 [==============================] - 0s 3ms/sample - loss:
0.0560 - accuracy: 1.0000
Test Score: 0.0560462586581707
Test Accuracy: 1.0
```

The output shows that our model achieved 100 percent accuracy on the test set.

Let's now plot the accuracy for 50 epochs.

Script 30:

```
1.   import matplotlib.pyplot as plt
2.
3.   plt.plot(model_history.history['accuracy'], label =
     'accuracy')
4.   plt.plot(model_history.history['val_accuracy'], label =
     'val_accuracy')
5.   plt.legend(['train','test'], loc='lower left')
```

Output:

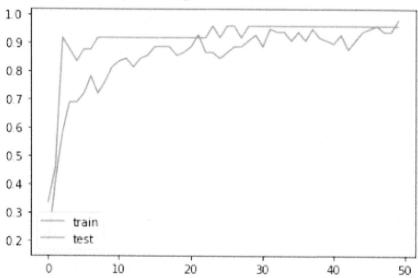

The result shows that on the training set, our model converged at around the 45th epoch. The final training and test accuracies are almost identical. Therefore, we can say that our model is not overfitting.

The following script plots the loss values for the training and test sets.

Script 31:

```
1.  import matplotlib.pyplot as plt
2.
3.  plt.plot(model_history.history['loss'], label = 'loss')
4.  plt.plot(model_history.history['val_loss'], label = 'val_
    loss')
5.  plt.legend(['train','test'], loc='upper left')
```

Output:

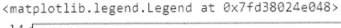

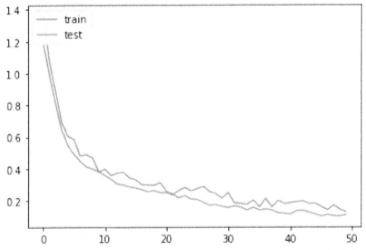

Now you know how to create densely connected neural networks for both binary and multiclass classification tasks. In the next section, you will see how to create a densely connected neural network for regression tasks.

4.4. Neural Network in TensorFlow for Regression

In regression tasks, you have to predict a continuous value, for instance, the price of the house, the score of a student in a particular exam, the quality of the wine, etc.

Creating a neural network for classification and regression tasks is quite similar. Here are the main differences:

1. There is no need to specify the activation function for the final dense layer, unlike classification tasks where you either use Sigmoid or Softmax activation function.

2. The loss function used should not be binary or categorical cross-entropy. Rather, you can use mean squared error as the loss function. You can also use stochastic gradient descent, etc.

3. The evaluation metrics for regression tasks cannot be accurate. You should use mean squared error, mean absolute error, or root mean squared error for the evaluation of neural network performance for regression.

§ Importing Required Libraries

The following script imports the required libraries.

Script 32:

```
1.  import seaborn as sns
2.  import pandas as pd
3.  import numpy as np
4.
5.  from tensorflow.keras.layers import Dense, Dropout,
    Activation
6.  from tensorflow.keras.models import Model, Sequential
7.  from tensorflow.keras.optimizers import Adam
```

§ Importing the Dataset

The following script imports the dataset for this section.

Output:

```
1.   wine_quality = pd.read_csv("https://raw.githubusercontent.
     com/shrikant-temburwar/Wine-Quality-Dataset/master/
     winequality-white.csv", sep=';')
```

Script 33:

```
1.   wine_quality.head()
```

Output:

	fixed acidity	volatile acidity	citric acid	residual sugar	chlorides	free sulfur dioxide	total sulfur dioxide	density	pH	sulphates	alcohol	quality
0	7.0	0.27	0.36	20.7	0.045	45.0	170.0	1.0010	3.00	0.45	8.8	6
1	6.3	0.30	0.34	1.6	0.049	14.0	132.0	0.9940	3.30	0.49	9.5	6
2	8.1	0.28	0.40	6.9	0.050	30.0	97.0	0.9951	3.26	0.44	10.1	6
3	7.2	0.23	0.32	8.5	0.058	47.0	186.0	0.9956	3.19	0.40	9.9	6
4	7.2	0.23	0.32	8.5	0.058	47.0	186.0	0.9956	3.19	0.40	9.9	6

The dataset contains records that contain information about white wines. The record contains features such as fixed acidity, volatile acidity, residual sugar, etc., along with the quality of wine on a scale of 1 to 10. The task is to predict the wine quality based on the remaining features.

The following script divides the data into features and target labels.

Script 34:

```
1.   X = wine_quality.drop(['quality'], axis=1).values
2.   y = wine_quality[['quality']].values
```

Dividing the Data into Training and Test Sets

The following script divides the data into the training and test sets.

Script 35:

```
1.   from sklearn.model_selection import train_test_split
2.   X_train, X_test, y_train, y_test = train_test_split(X, y,
     test_size=0.20, random_state=42)
```

And the following script performs data normalization.

Script 36:

```
1.  from sklearn.preprocessing import StandardScaler
2.  sc = StandardScaler()
3.  X_train = sc.fit_transform(X_train)
4.  X_test = sc.transform(X_test)
```

§ Creating a Neural Network Model for Regression

The following script defines a method **create_model_regression()**, which returns a Sequential model with three dense layers. The model contains four dense layers. The first three layers have 100, 50, and 25 nodes, respectively, while the final dense layer, which is also the output layer, contains only one neuron since we are predicting single regression value. The loss function in the compile method is **mean_squared_error**, while the metrics we use is the mean absolute error.

Script 37:

```
1.  def create_model_regression(learning_rate, dropout_rate):
2.
3.      model = Sequential()
4.      model.add(Dense(100, input_dim=X_train.shape[1],
    activation='relu'))
5.      model.add(Dropout(dropout_rate))
6.      model.add(Dense(50, activation='relu'))
7.      model.add(Dropout(dropout_rate))
8.      model.add(Dense(25, activation='relu'))
9.      model.add(Dropout(dropout_rate))
10.     model.add(Dense(1))
11.
12.     adam = Adam(lr=learning_rate)
13.     model.compile(loss='mean_squared_error',
    optimizer=adam, metrics=['mae'])
14.     return model
```

The following script defines the batch size, epochs, dropout, and learning rate.

Script 38:

```
1.  dropout_rate = 0.1
2.  epochs = 50
3.  batch_size = 1
4.  learn_rate = 0.001
```

Finally, the script below creates neural network model for regression by calling the **create_model_regression()** method. The architecture of the model is displayed in the output:

Script 39:

```
1.  model = create_model_regression(learn_rate, dropout_rate)
2.  from tensorflow.keras.utils import plot_model
3.  plot_model(model, to_file='model_plot1.png', show_
    shapes=True, show_layer_names=True)
```

Output:

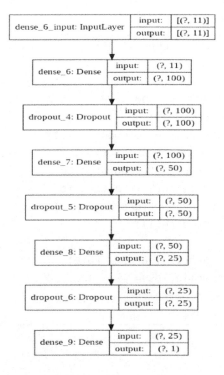

To train the model, again we need to call the **fit** method as shown below:

Script 40:

```
1.  model_history = model.fit(X_train, y_train, batch_
    size=batch_size, epochs=epochs, validation_split=0.2,
    verbose=1)
```

Output:

```
Epoch 45/50
3134/3134 [==============================] - 10s 3ms/sample - loss: 0.3416 - mae: 0.4475 - val_loss: 0.4684 - val_mae: 0.5139
Epoch 46/50
3134/3134 [==============================] - 10s 3ms/sample - loss: 0.3382 - mae: 0.4462 - val_loss: 0.4777 - val_mae: 0.5140
Epoch 47/50
3134/3134 [==============================] - 11s 3ms/sample - loss: 0.3407 - mae: 0.4439 - val_loss: 0.4795 - val_mae: 0.5140
Epoch 48/50
3134/3134 [==============================] - 11s 3ms/sample - loss: 0.3276 - mae: 0.4421 - val_loss: 0.4620 - val_mae: 0.5104
Epoch 49/50
3134/3134 [==============================] - 11s 4ms/sample - loss: 0.3359 - mae: 0.4404 - val_loss: 0.4764 - val_mae: 0.5217
Epoch 50/50
3134/3134 [==============================] - 10s 3ms/sample - loss: 0.3334 - mae: 0.4392 - val_loss: 0.4758 - val_mae: 0.5196
```

The output shows that the mean absolute error of 0.51 is achieved on the training set.

§ Evaluating the Neural Network Performance

The following script evaluates the performance of our regression model.

Script 41:

```
1.  accuracies = model.evaluate(X_test, y_test, verbose=1)
2.
3.  print("Test Score:", accuracies[0])
4.  print("Test Accuracy:", accuracies[1])
```

Output:

```
980/980 [==============================] - 0s 169us/sample -
loss: 0.5045 - mae: 0.5312
Test Score: 0.5045385690367952
Test Accuracy: 0.53124046
```

A mean absolute error value of 0.53 is obtained on the test set.

Finally, we can plot the mean absolute error values for the training and test sets.

Script 42:

```
1.  import matplotlib.pyplot as plt
2.
3.  plt.plot(model_history.history['mae'], label = 'mae')
4.  plt.plot(model_history.history['val_mae'], label = 'val_
    mae')
5.  plt.legend(['train','test'], loc='lower left')
```

Output:

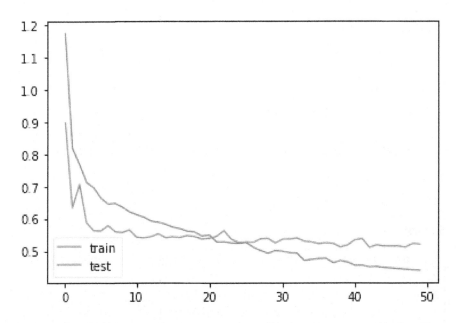

Since the MAE value for the training set is a little less than the test set, we can say that our model is overfitting. To reduce overfitting, try to increase the dropout rate.

Exercise 4.1

Question 1:

Which of the following loss functions can be used for regression problems:

1. Binary Cross-Entropy
2. Categorical Cross-Entropy
3. Log Likelihood
4. None of the Above

Question 2:

We say that a model is overfitting when:

1. Results on the test set are better than the results on the training set
2. Results on both the test and training sets are similar
3. Results on the training set are better than results on the test set
4. None of the above

Question 3:

In the output layer, the number of neurons depends upon:

1. The type of problem
2. The number of possible outputs
3. The activation function
4. The loss function

Exercise 4.2

```
1.  import seaborn as sns
2.  import pandas as pd
3.  import numpy as np
4.
5.  from tensorflow.keras.layers import Dense, Dropout,
    Activation
6.  from tensorflow.keras.models import Model, Sequential
7.  from tensorflow.keras.optimizers import Adam
8.
9.  diamond_data = sns.load_dataset('diamonds')
10.
11. diamond_data .head()
```

	carat	cut	color	clarity	depth	table	price	x	y	z
0	0.23	Ideal	E	SI2	61.5	55.0	326	3.95	3.98	2.43
1	0.21	Premium	E	SI1	59.8	61.0	326	3.89	3.84	2.31
2	0.23	Good	E	VS1	56.9	65.0	327	4.05	4.07	2.31
3	0.29	Premium	I	VS2	62.4	58.0	334	4.20	4.23	2.63
4	0.31	Good	J	SI2	63.3	58.0	335	4.34	4.35	2.75

From the diamond dataset above, predict the price of diamond using all the other features.

Tip: Use one-hot encoding to convert categorical variables into numerical variables.

5

Convolutional Neural Networks

5.1. Introduction

In the preceding chapter, you examined how to develop simple, densely connected neural networks for classification and regression tasks. Densely connected neural networks are the simplest of all the neural networks, where all the neurons in the previous layers are connected to all the neurons in the next layer. Such a neural network is useful when the input data is tabular. However, for more advanced problems where input data is not tabular, e.g., images, text, voice notes, and sequential data, more sophisticated neural networks have been developed. Convolutional neural network (CNN) is one such neural network.

A CNN is a type of neural network used to classify spatial data. For instance, images, sequences, etc. In an image, each pixel is somehow related to some other pictures. Looking at a single pixel, you cannot guess the image. Rather you have to look at the complete picture to guess the image. A CNN does exactly that. Using a kernel or feature, it detects features within an image. A combination of these images then forms the complete image, which can then be classified using a densely connected neural network. The steps involved in a Convolutional Neural Network have been explained in the next section.

5.2. Image Classification with CNN

In this chapter, you will see how to perform image classification using CNN. Before we go ahead and see the steps involved in the image classification using a convolutional neural network, we first need to know how computers see images.

5.2.1. How Do Computers See Images?

When humans see an image, they see lines, circles, squares, and different shapes. However, a computer sees an image differently. For a computer, an image is no more than a 2-D set of pixels arranged in a certain manner. For greyscale images, the pixel value can be between 0–255, while for color, here are three channels: red, green, and blue. Each channel can have a pixel value between 0–255.

Look at the following image 5.1.

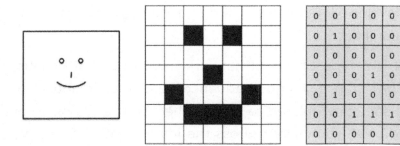

Image 5.1: How computers see images

Here, the box on the left most is what humans see. They see a smiling face. However, a computer sees it in the form of pixel values of 0s and 1s, as shown on the right-hand side. Here, 0 indicates a white pixel, whereas 1 indicates a black pixel. In the real world, 1 indicates a white pixel, while 0 indicates a black pixel.

Now, we know how a computer sees images. The next step is to explain the steps involved in the image classification using a convolutional neural network.

The following are the steps involved in image classification with CNN.

1. The Convolution Operation
2. The ReLu Operation
3. The Pooling Operation
4. Flattening and Fully Connected Layer

5.2.2. The Convolution Operation

The convolution operation is the first step involved in the image classification with a convolutional neural network.

In convolution operation, you have an image and a feature detector. The values of the feature detector are initialized randomly. The feature detector is moved over the image from left to right. The values in the feature detector are multiplied by the corresponding values in the image, and then all the values in the feature detector are added. The resultant value is added in the feature map.

Look at the following image, for example:

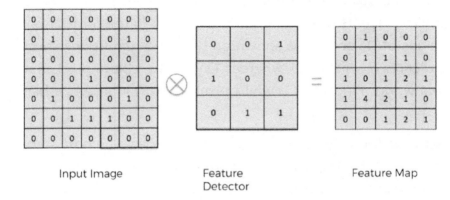

Input Image   Feature Detector   Feature Map

In the above script, we have an input image of 7 x 7. The feature detector is of size 3 x 3. The feature detector is placed over the image at the top left of the input image, and then the pixel values in the feature detector are multiplied by the pixel values in the input image. The result is then added. The feature detector then moves to N step toward right. Here, N refers to stride. A stride is basically the number of steps that a feature detector takes from left to right and then from top to bottom to find a new value for the feature map.

In reality, there are multiple feature detectors. As shown in the following image:

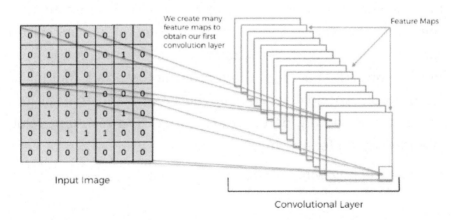

Input Image   Convolutional Layer

Each feature detector is responsible for detecting a particular feature in the image.

5.2.3. The ReLu Operation

In ReLu operation, you simply apply the ReLu activation function on the feature map generated as a result of the convolution operation. Convolution operation gives us linear values. The ReLu operation is performed to introduce non-linearity in the image.

In the ReLu operation, all the negative values in a feature map are replaced by 0. All the positive values are left untouched.

Suppose we have the following feature map:

-4	2	1	-2
1	-1	8	0
3	-3	1	4
1	0	1	-2

When the ReLu function is applied on the feature map, the resultant feature map looks like this:

0	2	1	0
1	-0	8	0
3	0	1	4
1	0	1	0

5.2.4. The Pooling Operation

Pooling operation is performed in order to introduce spatial invariance in the feature map. Pooling operation is performed after convolution and ReLu operation.

Let's first understand what spatial invariance is. If you look at the following three images, you can easily identify that these images contain cheetahs.

Although the second image is disoriented and the third image is distorted, we are still able to identify that all the three images contain cheetahs based on certain features.

Pooling does exactly that. In pooling, we have a feature map and then a pooling filter which can be of any size. Next, we move the pooling filter over the feature map and apply the pooling operation. There can be many pooling operations such as max pooling, min pooling, and average pooling. In max pooling, we choose the maximum value from the pooling filter. Pooling not only introduces spatial invariance but also reduces the size of an image.

Look at the following image. Here in the 3rd and 4th rows and 1st and 2nd columns, we have four values 1, 0, 1, 4. When we apply max pooling on these four pixels, the maximum value will be chosen, i.e., you can see 4 in the pooled feature map.

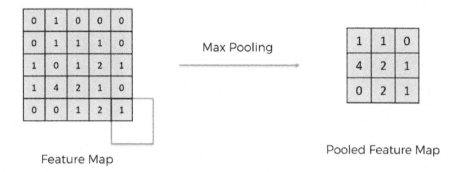

Feature Map   Max Pooling   Pooled Feature Map

5.2.5.   Flattening and Fully Connected Layer

To find more features from an image, the pooled feature maps are flattened to form a one-dimensional vector, as shown in the following figure:

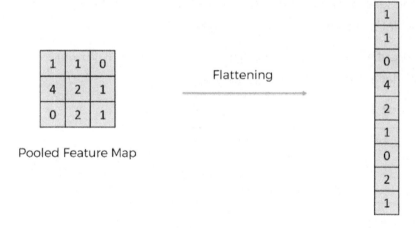

Pooled Feature Map   Flattening

The one-dimensional vector is then used as input to densely or fully connected neural network layer that you saw in Chapter 4. This is shown in the following image:

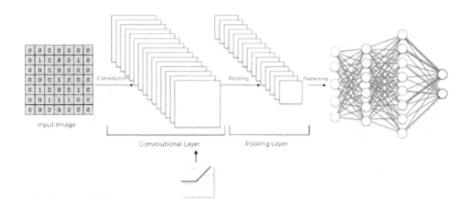

5.2.6. Implementing CNN With TensorFlow Keras

In this section, you will see how to implement CNN for Image Classification in TensorFlow Keras. We will create a CNN that is able to classify an image of fashion items such as shirts, pants, trousers, and sandals into one of the 10 predefined categories. So, let's begin without much ado.

Execute the following script to make sure that you are running the latest version of TensorFlow.

Script 1:

```
1.  !pip install --upgrade tensorflow
2.
3.  import tensorflow as tf
4.  print(tf.__version__)
```

Output:

```
2.2.0-rc1
```

The following script imports the required libraries and classes.

Script 2:

```
1.    import numpy as np
2.    import matplotlib.pyplot as plt
3.    from tensorflow.keras.layers import Input, Conv2D, Dense,
      Flatten, Dropout, MaxPool2D
4.    from tensorflow.keras.models import Model
```

The following script downloads the Fashion MNIST dataset that contains images of different fashion items along with their labels. The script divides the data into training images and training labels and test images and test labels.

Script 3:

```
1.    mnist_data = tf.keras.datasets.fashion_mnist
2.
3.    (training_images, training_labels), (test_images, test_
      labels) = mnist_data .load_data()
```

Images in our dataset are greyscale images where each pixel value lies between 0 and 255. The following script normalizes pixel values between 0 and 1.

Script 4:

```
1.    training_images, test_images = training_images/255.0,
      test_images/255.0
```

Let's print the shape of our training data.

Script 5:

```
1.    print(training_images.shape)
```

Output:

```
(60000, 28, 28)
```

The above output shows that our training dataset contains 60 thousand records (images). Each image is 28 pixels wide and 28 pixels high.

Let's print an image randomly from the test set:

Script 6:

```
1.   plt.figure()
2.   plt.imshow(test_images[9])
3.   plt.colorbar()
4.   plt.grid(False)
5.   plt.show()
```

Output:

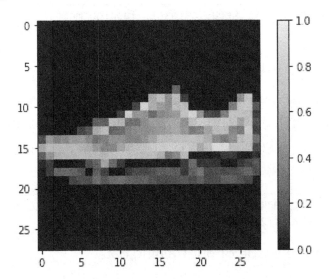

The output shows that the 9th image in our test set is the image of a sneaker.

The next step is to change the dimensions of our input images. CNN in Keras expect data to be in the format Width-Height-Channels. Our images contain width and height but no channels. Since the images are grayscale, we set the image channel to 1, as shown in the following script:

Script 7:

```
1.   training_images = np.expand_dims(training_images, -1)
2.   test_images = np.expand_dims(test_images, -1)
3.   print(training_images.shape)
```

Output:

```
(60000, 28, 28, 1)
```

The next step is to find the number of output classes. This number will be used to define the number of neurons in the output layer.

Script 8:

```
1.   output_classes = len(set(training_labels))
2.   print("Number of output classes is: ", output_classes)
```

Output:

```
Number of output classes is:   10
```

As expected, the number of output classes in our dataset is 10.

Let's print the shape of a single image in the training set.

Script 9:

```
1.   training_images[0].shape
```

Output:

```
(28, 28, 1)
```

The shape of a single image is (28, 28, 1). This shape will be used to train our convolutional neural network. The following script creates a model for our convolutional neural network.

Script 10:

```
1.  input_layer = Input(shape = training_images[0].shape )
2.  conv1 = Conv2D(32, (3,3), strides = 2, activation= 'relu')
    (input_layer)
3.  maxpool1 = MaxPool2D(2, 2)(conv1)
4.  conv2 = Conv2D(64, (3,3), strides = 2, activation= 'relu')
    (maxpool1)
5.  #conv3 = Conv2D(128, (3,3), strides = 2, activation=
    'relu')(conv2)
6.  flat1 = Flatten()(conv2)
7.  drop1 = Dropout(0.2)(flat1)
8.  dense1 = Dense(512, activation = 'relu')(drop1)
9.  drop2  = Dropout(0.2)(dense1)
10. output_layer = Dense(output_classes, activation=
    'softmax')(drop2)
11.
12. model = Model(input_layer, output_layer)
```

The model contains one input layer, two convolutional layers, one flattening layer, one hidden dense layer, and one output layer. The number of filters in the first convolutional layer is 32, while the second convolutional layer is 64. The kernel size for both convolutional layers is 3 x 3, with a stride of 2. After the first convolutional layer, a max pooling layer with a size 2 x 2 and stride 2 has also been defined.

It is important to mention that while defining the model layers, we used Keras Functional API. With Keras functional API, to connect the previous layer with the next layer, the name of the previous layer is passed inside the parenthesis at the end of the next layer.

The following line compiles the model.

Script 11:

```
1.  model.compile(optimizer = 'adam', loss= 'sparse_
    categorical_crossentropy', metrics =['accuracy'])
```

Finally, execute the following script to print the model architecture.

Script 12:

```
1.  from tensorflow.keras.utils import plot_model
2.  plot_model(model, to_file='model_plot1.png', show_
    shapes=True, show_layer_names=True)
```

Output:

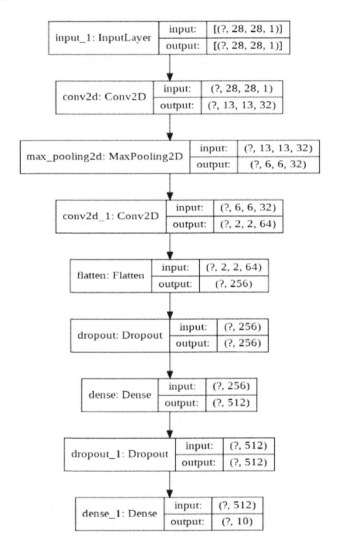

The following script trains the image classification model.

Script 13:

```
1.  model_history = model.fit(training_images, training_labels,
    epochs=20, validation_data=(test_images, test_labels),
    verbose=1)
```

The results from the last five epochs are shown in the output.

Output:

```
Epoch 16/20
1875/1875 [==============================] - 5s 2ms/step - loss: 0.2318 - accuracy: 0.9107 - val_loss: 0.3217 - val_accuracy: 0.8843
Epoch 17/20
1875/1875 [==============================] - 4s 2ms/step - loss: 0.2269 - accuracy: 0.9129 - val_loss: 0.3268 - val_accuracy: 0.8870
Epoch 18/20
1875/1875 [==============================] - 4s 2ms/step - loss: 0.2224 - accuracy: 0.9147 - val_loss: 0.3379 - val_accuracy: 0.8814
Epoch 19/20
1875/1875 [==============================] - 4s 2ms/step - loss: 0.2164 - accuracy: 0.9174 - val_loss: 0.3279 - val_accuracy: 0.8846
Epoch 20/20
1875/1875 [==============================] - 4s 2ms/step - loss: 0.2112 - accuracy: 0.9192 - val_loss: 0.3277 - val_accuracy: 0.8882
```

Let's plot the training and test accuracies for our model.

Script 14:

```
1.  import matplotlib.pyplot as plt
2.
3.  plt.plot(model_history.history['accuracy'], label =
    'accuracy')
4.  plt.plot(model_history.history['val_accuracy'], label =
    'val_accuracy')
5.  plt.legend(['train','test'], loc='lower left')
```

The following output shows that training accuracy is higher, and test accuracy starts to flatten after 88 percent. We can say that our model is overfitting.

Output:

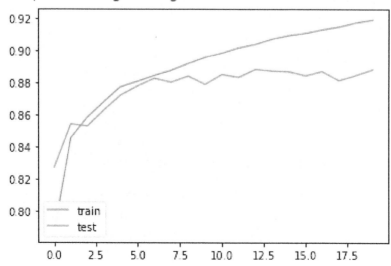

<matplotlib.legend.Legend at 0x7feb3006b4e0>

Let's make a prediction on one of the images in the test set. Let's predict the label for image 9. We know that image 9 contains a sneaker, as we saw earlier by plotting the image.

Script 15:

```
1.  output = model.predict(test_images)
2.  prediction = np.argmax(output[9])
3.  print(prediction)
```

Output:

7

The output shows number 7. The output will always be a number since deep learning algorithms work only with numbers. The numbers correspond to the following labels.

0: T-shirt\top

1: Trouser

2: Pullover

3: Dress

4: Coat

5: Sandal

6: Shirt

7: Sneaker

8: Bag

9: Ankle boot

The above list shows that number 7 corresponds to sneakers. Hence, the prediction by our CNN is correct.

In this chapter, you saw an application of a convolutional neural network for image classification. CNN is also used for sequence problems such as sentence classification and stock market prediction. In chapter 7, you will see how a 1-dimensional convolutional neural network can be used for sentiment classification task from text reviews.

Exercise 5.1

Question 1

What should be the input shape of the input image to the convolutional neural network?

1.   Width, Height
2.   Height, Width
3.   Channels, Width, Height
4.   Width, Height, Channels

Question 2

The pooling layer is used to pick correct features even if:

1.   Image is Inverted
2.   Image is distorted
3.   Image is compressed
4.   All of the above

Question 3

The ReLu activation function is used to introduce:

1.   Linearity
2.   Non-linearity
3.   Quadraticity
4.   None of the above

Exercise 5.2

Using the CFAR 10 image dataset, perform image classification to recognize an image. Here is the dataset :

```
1.  cifar_dataset = tf.keras.datasets.cifar10
```

6

Sequence Classification with Recurrent Neural Networks (RNN)

6.1. What Is an RNN and LSTM?

This section explains what a recurrent neural network (RNN) is, what is the problem with RNN, and how a long short-term memory network (LSTM) can be used to solve the problems with RNN.

6.1.1. What Is an RNN?

A recurrent neural network, also labeled RNN, is a type of neural network that is used to process data that is sequential in nature. Sequential data is a type of data where the value of data at time step T depends upon the values of data at time steps less than T. For instance, sound waves, text sentences, stock market prices, etc. In the stock market price prediction problem, the value of the opening price of a stock at a given data depends upon the opening stock price of the previous days.

The difference between the architecture of a recurrent neural network and a simple neural network is presented in the following figure:

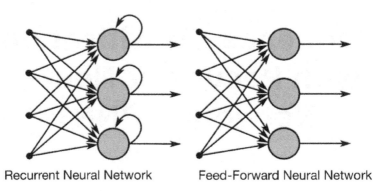

Recurrent Neural Network   Feed-Forward Neural Network

In a recurrent neural network, at each time step, the previous output of the neuron is also multiplied by the current input via a weight vector. From the above figure, it is plain that the output from a neuron is looped back into for the next time step. The following figure makes this concept further clear:

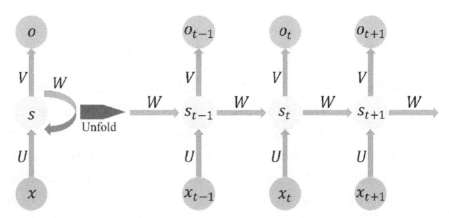

Here, we have a single neuron with one input and one output. On the right side, the process followed by a recurrent neural network is unfolded. You can see that at time step t, the input

is multiplied by weight vector U, while the previous output at time t-1, i.e., St-1 is multiplied by the weight vector W, the sum of the input vector XU + SW becomes the output at time T. This is how a recurrent neural network captures the sequential information.

6.1.2. Problems with RNN

A problem with the recurrent neural network is that while it can capture a shorter sequence, it tends to forget longer sequences.

For instance, it is easier to predict the missing word in the following sentence because the Keyword "Birds" is present in the same sentence.

"Birds fly in the ___."

RNN can easily guess that the missing word is "Clouds" here.

However, RNN cannot remember longer sequences such as this one ...

"Mike grew up in France. He likes to eat cheese, he plays piano .... and he speaks _____ fluently".

Here, the RNN can only guess that the missing word is "French" if it remembers the first sentence, i.e., "Mike grew up in France."

The recurrent neural networks consist of multiple recurrent layers, which results in a diminishing gradient problem. The diminishing gradient problem is that during the backpropagation of the recurrent layer, the gradient of the earlier layer becomes infinitesimally small, which virtually stops the initial layers of a neural network from learning anything.

To solve this problem, a special type of recurrent neural network, i.e., Long Short-Term Memory (LSTM) has been developed.

6.1.3. What Is an LSTM?

LSTM is a type of RNN which is capable of remembering longer sequences, and hence, is one of the most commonly used RNN for sequence tasks.

In LSTM, instead of a single unit in the recurrent cell, there are four interacting units, i.e., a forget gate, an input gate, an update gate, and an output gate. The overall architecture of an LSTM cell is shown in the following figure:

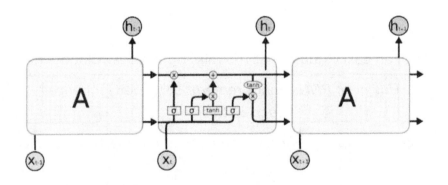

LSTM: Single Input - Single Output

Let's briefly discuss all the components of LSTM:

Cell State

The cell state In LSTM is responsible for remembering a long sequence. The following figure describes the cell state:

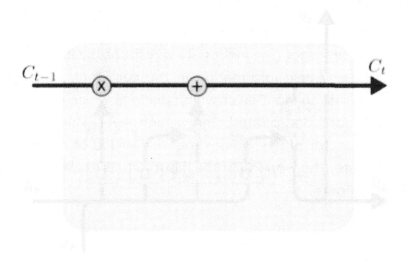

The cell state contains data from all the previous cells in the sequence. The LSTM is capable of adding or removing information to a cell state. In other words, LSTM tells the cell state which part of previous information to remember and which information to forget.

Forget Gate

The forget gate basically tells the cell state which information to retain from the information in the previous step and which information to forget. The working and calculation formula for the forget gate is as follows:

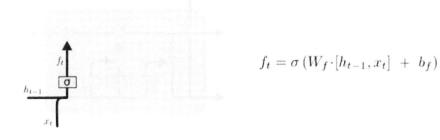

$$f_t = \sigma \left(W_f \cdot [h_{t-1}, x_t] + b_f \right)$$

Input Gate

The forget gate is used to decide which information to remember or forget. The input gate is responsible for updating or adding any new information in the cell state. Input gate has two parts: an input layer which decides which part of the cell state is to be updated, and a tanh layer which actually creates a vector of new values that are added or replaced in the cell state. The working of the input gate is explained in the following figure:

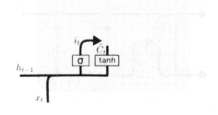

$$i_t = \sigma\left(W_i \cdot [h_{t-1}, x_t] + b_i\right)$$
$$\tilde{C}_t = \tanh(W_C \cdot [h_{t-1}, x_t] + b_C)$$

Update Gate

The forget tells what to forget and the input gate tells what to add to the cell state. The next step is to actually perform these two operations. The update gate is basically used to perform these two operations. The functioning and the equations for the update gate are as follows:

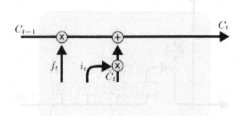

$$C_t = f_t * C_{t-1} + i_t * \tilde{C}_t$$

Output Gate

Finally, you have the output gate which outputs a hidden state and the output, just like a common recurrent neural network. The additional output from an LSTM node is cell state which runs between all the nodes in a sequence. The equations and the functioning of the output gate are depicted by the following figure:

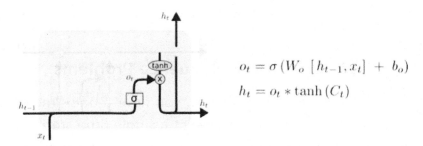

$$o_t = \sigma \left(W_o \left[h_{t-1}, x_t \right] + b_o \right)$$
$$h_t = o_t * \tanh \left(C_t \right)$$

In the following sections, you will see how to use LSTM to solve different types of Sequence problems.

6.2. Types of Sequence Problems

Sequence problems can be broadly classified into four categories:

1. One to One Sequence Problems

2. One to Many Sequence Problems

3. Many to One Sequence Problems

4. Many to Many Sequence Problems

The following figure differentiates between different types of sequence problems.

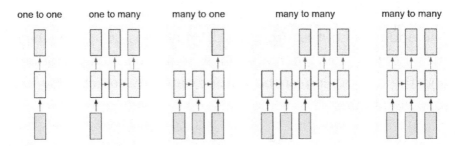

6.2.1. One to One Sequence Problems

In one to one sequence problems, you have a one-time step in the input, and you have to predict a single time step in the output. A perfect example of one to one sequence problem is image labeling, where you have an image as input, and you have to find the label for the image or the name for the image.

Let's see a simple example of solving one to one sequence problems with LSTM using Keras library.

We will be using the Google Colab notebook to run the scripts in this Chapter. The detailed explanation for how to run scripts via the Google Colab is given in chapter 1.

The first action we will take is upgrade the TensorFlow library to the latest version by executing the following script.

Script 1:

```
1.  pip install --upgrade tensorflow
```

You must have a TensorFlow version > 2.0 in order to run the scripts in this chapter. You can check the TensorFlow version using the following command.

Script 2:

```
1.  import tensorflow as tf
2.  print(tf.__version__)
```

Output:

```
2.2.0-rc3
```

Next, we will import the libraries required to run the scripts in this section.

Script 3:

```
1.  import numpy as np
2.  import matplotlib.pyplot as plt
3.  from tensorflow.keras.layers import Input, Activation,
    Dense, Flatten, Dropout,  Flatten, LSTM
4.  from tensorflow.keras.models import Model
```

Let's create our dataset. In our dataset, our input feature set will have a single time step and two features per time step. The following script creates our feature set X and the label set y.

Script 4:

```
1.  X1 = list()
2.  X2 = list()
3.
4.  X = list()
5.  y = list()
6.
7.  X1 = [(x+1)*4 for x in range(25)]
8.  X2 = [(x+1)*5 for x in range(25)]
9.
10. y = [x1*x2 for x1,x2 in zip(X1,X2)]
11.
12. y = np.array(y)
```

Let's print our feature set and labels.

Script 5:

```
1.  X = np.column_stack((X1, X2))
2.  print(X)
3.  print(y)
```

Output:

```
[[  4   5]
 [  8  10]
 [ 12  15]
 [ 16  20]
 [ 20  25]
 [ 24  30]
 [ 28  35]
 [ 32  40]
 [ 36  45]
 [ 40  50]
 [ 44  55]
 [ 48  60]
 [ 52  65]
 [ 56  70]
 [ 60  75]
 [ 64  80]
 [ 68  85]
 [ 72  90]
 [ 76  95]
 [ 80 100]
 [ 84 105]
 [ 88 110]
 [ 92 115]
 [ 96 120]
 [100 125]]
[    20    80   180   320   500   720   980  1280  1620  2000
  2420  2880  3380  3920  4500  5120  5780  6480  7220  8000
  8820  9680 10580 11520 12500]
```

You can see that each record in the feature set consists of two features. The first feature contains a value that is a multiple of 4, and the second feature contains a value which is a multiple of 5. The output label simply contains the product of two features.

The LSTM in TensorFlow Keras library expects the dataset to be in three-dimensional shape, i.e., number of Records, time step per record, and features per time step. We have 25 records in the input feature set with one time step and two features per time step. The following script reshapes our input feature set.

Script 6:

```
1.   X = np.array(X).reshape(25, 1, 2)
2.   X.shape
```

Output:

```
(25, 1, 2)
```

Finally, now we can create our LSTM neural network. The first layer is the input layer where we specify the shape of each record. Each record consists of one time step and 2 features per time step.

Next, we create three LSTM layers with 100, 50, and 25 nodes. The activation layer used is the ReLu layer. Finally, we have a dense layer with 10 nodes and an output layer, which is also a dense layer, with 1 node since we want to predict a single value.

Script 7:

```
1.  input_layer = Input(shape = (1,2))
2.  lstm1 = LSTM(100, activation='relu', return_
    sequences=True)(input_layer)
3.  lstm2 = LSTM(50, activation='relu', return_sequences=True)
    (lstm1)
4.  lstm3 = LSTM(25, activation='relu') (lstm2)
5.  dense1 = Dense(10, activation='relu')(lstm3)
6.  output_layer = Dense(1)(dense1)
7.  model = Model(input_layer, output_layer)
8.  model.compile(optimizer='adam', loss='mse')
```

Let's plot our neural network.

Script 8:

```
1.  from tensorflow.keras.utils import plot_model
2.  plot_model(model, to_file='model_plot1.png', show_
    shapes=True, show_layer_names=True)
```

Output:

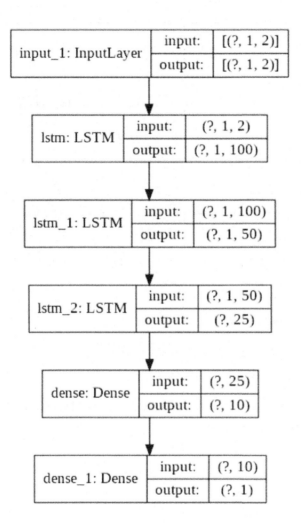

You can see that the input has one time step with two features, and the final layer has a single output. The following script trains our model.

Script 9:

```
1.  model_history = model.fit(X, y, epochs=1000, verbose=1)
```

The output below shows the loss value at the end of the 1000th epoch.

Output:

```
Epoch 997/1000
1/1 [==============================] - 0s 3ms/step - loss:
3009.5291
Epoch 998/1000
1/1 [==============================] - 0s 1ms/step - loss:
2981.4268
Epoch 999/1000
1/1 [==============================] - 0s 784us/step - loss:
2954.3359
Epoch 1000/1000
1/1 [==============================] - 0s 1ms/step - loss:
2950.4763
```

We can also plot the loss with the help of the following script:

Script 10:

```
1.   import matplotlib.pyplot as plt
2.
3.   plt.plot(model_history.history['loss'], label = 'loss')
4.   plt.legend(['train'], loc='top right')
```

You can see that the loss decreases till the 200th epoch, and then the curve flattens out.

Output:

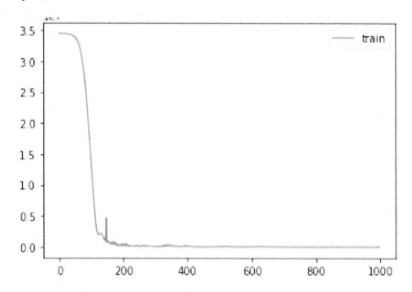

Let's now make a prediction on single record. Our test record has two features 104 and 130. Hence, the actual output should be the product of these two numbers, i.e. 13,520.

Script 11:

```
1.  X_test = np.array([104,130]) # 13520
2.  X_test = X_test.reshape((1, 1, 2))
3.  y_pred = model.predict(X_test, verbose=0)
4.  print(y_pred)
```

Output:

```
[[13229.459]]
```

The output shows that our model predicted 13,229 as the product of 104,130 which is pretty close to 13,250.

6.2.2. Many to One Sequence Problems

In many to one problem, we have multiple time steps in the input feature set but a single value in the output. Text classification is a classic example of many to one sequence problems. For example, the input to the model is a sentence or a sequence of words, and the output is the sentiment of the text such as happy, sad, neutral, etc.

Let's see an example of how to solve many to one sequence problems with Keras. Let's first create our feature set. Our input dataset will have two features. The first feature consists of multiples of 4 from 4 to 160, whereas the second feature consists of multiples of 5 from 5 to 200.

Script 12:

```
1.   X1 = np.array([x+4 for x in range(0, 160, 4)])
2.   print(X1)
3.
4.   X2 = np.array([x+5 for x in range(0, 200, 5)])
5.   print(X2)
```

Output:

```
[  4   8  12  16  20  24  28  32  36  40  44  48  52  56  60
 64  68  72  76  80  84  88  92  96 100 104 108 112 116 120 124
128 132 136 140 144 148 152 156 160]
[  5  10  15  20  25  30  35  40  45  50  55  60  65  70  75
 80  85  90  95 100 105 110 115 120 125 130 135 140 145 150 155
160 165 170 175 180  185 190 195 200]
```

Next, we stack our two features together.

Script 13:

```
1.   X = np.column_stack((X1, X2))
2.   print(X)
```

Output:

```
[[  4   5]
 [  8  10]
 [ 12  15]
 [ 16  20]
 [ 20  25]
 [ 24  30]
 [ 28  35]
 [ 32  40]
 [ 36  45]
 [ 40  50]
 [ 44  55]
 [ 48  60]
 [ 52  65]
 [ 56  70]
 [ 60  75]
 [ 64  80]
 [ 68  85]
 [ 72  90]
 [ 76  95]
 [ 80 100]
 [ 84 105]
 [ 88 110]
 [ 92 115]
 [ 96 120]
 [100 125]
 [104 130]
 [108 135]
 [112 140]
 [116 145]
 [120 150]
 [124 155]
 [128 160]
 [132 165]
 [136 170]
 [140 175]
 [144 180]
 [148 185]
 [152 190]
 [156 195]
 [160 200]]
```

Finally, we reshape our feature set so that each record has two time steps, and one time step consists of two features.

Script 14:

```
1.  X = np.array(X).reshape(20, 2, 2)
2.  print(X)
```

Output:

```
1.   [[[  4   5]
2.    [  8  10]]
3.
4.     [[ 12  15]
5.      [ 16  20]]
6.
7.     [[ 20  25]
8.      [ 24  30]]
9.
10.    [[ 28  35]
11.     [ 32  40]]
12.
13.    [[ 36  45]
14.     [ 40  50]]
15.
16.    [[ 44  55]
17.     [ 48  60]]
18.
19.    [[ 52  65]
20.     [ 56  70]]
21.
22.    [[ 60  75]
23.     [ 64  80]]
24.
25.    [[ 68  85]
26.     [ 72  90]]
27.
28.    [[ 76  95]
29.     [ 80 100]]
30.
```

```
31.    [[ 84 105]
32.     [ 88 110]]
33.
34.    [[ 92 115]
35.     [ 96 120]]
36.
37.    [[100 125]
38.     [104 130]]
39.
40.    [[108 135]
41.     [112 140]]
42.
43.    [[116 145]
44.     [120 150]]
45.
46.    [[124 155]
47.     [128 160]]
48.
49.    [[132 165]
50.     [136 170]]
51.
52.    [[140 175]
53.     [144 180]]
54.
55.    [[148 185]
56.     [152 190]]
57.
58.    [[156 195]
59.     [160 200]]]
```

The output is simply the sum of two features in the two time steps for each input record.

Script 15:

```
1.    y = [sum (y) for y in [sum(x) for x in X]]
2.    y = np.array(y)
3.    print(y)
```

Output:

```
[ 27  63  99 135 171 207 243 279 315 351 387 423 459 495 531
567 603 639 675 711]
```

Next, we will create our neural network. This neural network is very similar to the one we created earlier in the previous section. However, the shape of the input layer is different here since we have two input steps instead of one and two features per input step.

Script 16:

```
1.   input_layer = Input(shape = (2,2))
2.   lstm1 = LSTM(100, activation='relu', return_
     sequences=True)(input_layer)
3.   lstm2 = LSTM(50, activation='relu', return_sequences=True)
     (lstm1)
4.   lstm3 = LSTM(25, activation='relu') (lstm2)
5.   dense1 = Dense(10, activation='relu')(lstm3)
6.   output_layer = Dense(1)(dense1)
7.   model = Model(input_layer, output_layer)
8.   model.compile(optimizer='adam', loss='mse')
```

The following script displays the architecture of our model.

Script 17:

```
1.   from tensorflow.keras.utils import plot_model
2.   plot_model(model, to_file='model_plot1.png', show_
     shapes=True, show_layer_names=True)
```

Output:

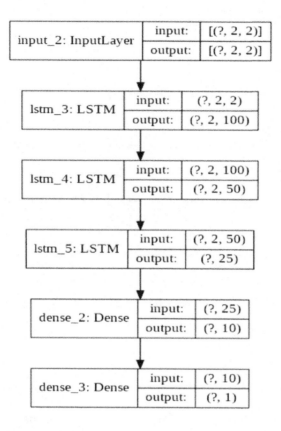

Finally, execute the following script to train the model.

Script 18:

```
1.  model_history = model.fit(X, y, epochs=1000, verbose=1)
```

The loss value achieved at the end of the 1000th epoch has been printed below:

Output:

```
Epoch 996/1000
1/1 [==============================] - 0s 1ms/step - loss:
0.0318
Epoch 997/1000
1/1 [==============================] - 0s 811us/step - loss:
0.0316
Epoch 998/1000
1/1 [==============================] - 0s 892us/step - loss:
0.0315
Epoch 999/1000
1/1 [==============================] - 0s 782us/step - loss:
0.0314
Epoch 1000/1000
1/1 [==============================] - 0s 766us/step - loss:
0.0313
```

We can also plot the values for the loss with respect to epochs using the following script.

Script 19:

```
1.  import matplotlib.pyplot as plt
2.
3.  plt.plot(model_history.history['loss'], label = 'loss')
4.  plt.legend(['train'], loc='top right')
```

Output:

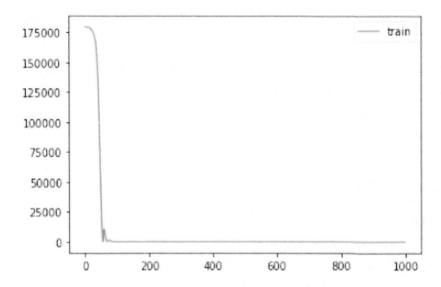

You can see that the minimum error value is achieved around the 60th epoch.

Let's test our code. We have a test record with two time steps and two features per time step. The actual output value is 859.

Script 20:

```
1.  X_test = np.array([[200, 225], ## 859
2.                     [204,230]])
3.  X_test = X_test.reshape((1, 2, 2))
4.  y_pred = model.predict(X_test, verbose=0)
5.  print(y_pred)
```

Our model predicts 860.60, which is extremely close to 859, which shows that our model is working perfectly fine.

Output:

```
[[860.6011]]
```

6.2.3. One to Many Sequence Problems

In one to many sequence problems, you have an input containing a single time step, whereas the output consists of multiple time steps. For instance, image to text description is a perfect example of one to many sequence problems where the input to LSTM is an image, and the output is the description of the image.

Let's create our dataset and print the input features and the output labels.

Script 21:

```
1.   X1 = list()
2.   X2 = list()
3.
4.   X = list()
5.   y = list()
6.
7.   X1 = [(x+1)*6 for x in range(30)]
8.   X2 = [(x+1)*7 for x in range(30)]
9.
10.  for x1, x2 in zip(X1, X2):
11.      output = list()
12.      output.append(x1-2)
13.      output.append(x2-3)
14.      y.append(output)
15.
16.  X = np.column_stack((X1, X2))
17.  print(X)
```

Output:

```
[[  6    7]
 [ 12   14]
 [ 18   21]
 [ 24   28]
 [ 30   35]
 [ 36   42]
 [ 42   49]
 [ 48   56]
 [ 54   63]
 [ 60   70]
 [ 66   77]
 [ 72   84]
 [ 78   91]
 [ 84   98]
 [ 90  105]
 [ 96  112]
 [102  119]
 [108  126]
 [114  133]
 [120  140]
 [126  147]
 [132  154]
 [138  161]
 [144  168]
 [150  175]
 [156  182]
 [162  189]
 [168  196]
 [174  203]
 [180  210]]
```

Script 22:

```
1.  print(y)
```

Output:

```
[[4, 4], [10, 11], [16, 18], [22, 25], [28, 32], [34, 39],
[40, 46], [46, 53], [52, 60], [58, 67], [64, 74], [70, 81],
[76, 88], [82, 95], [88, 102], [94, 109], [100, 116],
[106, 123], [112, 130], [118, 137], [124, 144], [130, 151],
[136, 158], [142, 165], [148, 172], [154, 179], [160, 186],
[166, 193], [172, 200], [178, 207]]
```

Next, we need to reshape our input feature set.

Script 23:

```
1.  X = np.array(X).reshape(30, 1, 2)
2.  y = np.array(y)
```

Finally, we can train our neural network. The neural network is similar to the neural network we had in the previous section. The only difference is that the following neural network has two nodes in the output layer, since the output label consists of two time steps.

Script 24:

```
1.  input_layer = Input(shape = (1,2))
2.  lstm1 = LSTM(100, activation='relu', return_
    sequences=True)(input_layer)
3.  lstm2 = LSTM(50, activation='relu', return_sequences=True)
    (lstm1)
4.  lstm3 = LSTM(25, activation='relu') (lstm2)
5.  dense1 = Dense(10, activation='relu')(lstm3)
6.  output_layer = Dense(2)(dense1)
7.  model = Model(input_layer, output_layer)
8.  model.compile(optimizer='adam', loss='mse')
```

The following script prints the architecture of our neural network.

Script 25:

```
1.   from tensorflow.keras.utils import plot_model
2.   plot_model(model, to_file='model_plot1.png', show_
     shapes=True, show_layer_names=True)
```

Output:

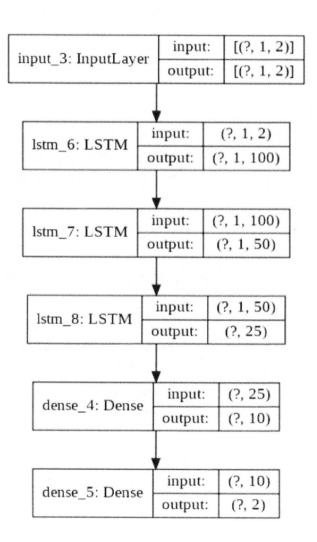

Finally, to train the LSTM model, execute the following script. The loss achieved after the 1000th epoch is printed in the output.

Script 26:

```
1.   model_history = model.fit(X, y, epochs=1000, verbose=1)
```

Output:

```
Epoch 996/1000
1/1 [==============================] - 0s 822us/step - loss:
0.0415
Epoch 997/1000
1/1 [==============================] - 0s 760us/step - loss:
0.0414
Epoch 998/1000
1/1 [==============================] - 0s 713us/step - loss:
0.0413
Epoch 999/1000
1/1 [==============================] - 0s 721us/step - loss:
0.0412
Epoch 1000/1000
1/1 [==============================] - 0s 743us/step - loss:
0.0411
```

To plot the loss against the number of epochs, run the following
script.

Script 27:

```
1.   import matplotlib.pyplot as plt
2.
3.   plt.plot(model_history.history['loss'], label = 'loss')
4.   plt.legend(['train'], loc='top right')
```

Output:

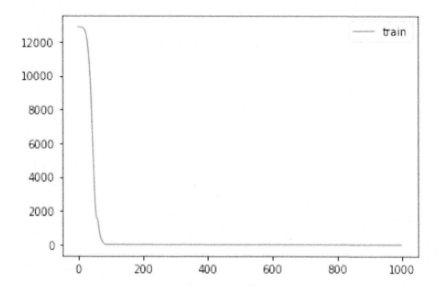

The output shows that the minimum value for loss is achieved after approximately 100 epochs.

The following example predicts the output for a test record. The actual output is 298, 347.

Script 28:

```
1.   X_test = np.array([300, 350])
2.   X_test = X_test.reshape((1, 1, 2))
3.   y_pred = model.predict(X_test, verbose=0)
4.   print(y_pred)
```

Output:

```
[[296.53806 344.72116]]
```

The predicted output is 296.54 and 344.72, which are pretty close to 298 and 347.

6.2.4. Many to Many Sequence Problems

In many to many sequence problems, both inputs and outputs consist of many time steps. One of the most common examples of a many to many systems is a chatbot. The input to a chatbot is a question that consists of a sequence of words, and the answer from the robot is another sequence of words.

Let's see an example of many to many sequence problems. The following script creates our dataset. Each time step in our input dataset consists of two features.

Script 29:

```
1.   X = list()
2.   y = list()
3.   X1 = [x1 for x1 in range(6, 361, 6)]
4.   X2 = [x2 for x2 in range(7, 421, 7)]
5.   y = [y for y in range(36, 391, 6)]
```

The following scripts print the features and labels set before they are reshaped.

Script 30:

```
1.   X = np.column_stack((X1, X2))
2.   y= np.array(y)
```

Script 31:

```
1.   print(X)
```

Output:

```
array([[  6,    7],
       [ 12,   14],
       [ 18,   21],
       [ 24,   28],
       [ 30,   35],
       [ 36,   42],
       [ 42,   49],
```

```
       [ 48,  56],
       [ 54,  63],
       [ 60,  70],
       [ 66,  77],
       [ 72,  84],
       [ 78,  91],
       [ 84,  98],
       [ 90, 105],
       [ 96, 112],
       [102, 119],
       [108, 126],
       [114, 133],
       [120, 140],
       [126, 147],
       [132, 154],
       [138, 161],
       [144, 168],
       [150, 175],
       [156, 182],
       [162, 189],
       [168, 196],
       [174, 203],
       [180, 210],
       [186, 217],
       [192, 224],
       [198, 231],
       [204, 238],
       [210, 245],
       [216, 252],
       [222, 259],
       [228, 266],
       [234, 273],
       [240, 280],
       [246, 287],
       [252, 294],
       [258, 301],
       [264, 308],
       [270, 315],
       [276, 322],
```

```
         [282, 329],
         [288, 336],
         [294, 343],
         [300, 350],
         [306, 357],
         [312, 364],
         [318, 371],
         [324, 378],
         [330, 385],
         [336, 392],
         [342, 399],
         [348, 406],
         [354, 413],
         [360, 420]])
```

Script 32:

```
1.  print(y)
```

Output:

```
array([ 36,  42,  48,  54,  60,  66,  72,  78,  84,  90,  96,
102, 108, 114, 120, 126, 132, 138, 144, 150, 156, 162, 168,
174, 180, 186, 192, 198, 204, 210, 216, 222, 228, 234, 240,
246, 252, 258, 264, 270, 276, 282, 288, 294, 300, 306, 312,
318, 324, 330, 336, 342, 348, 354, 360, 366, 372, 378, 384,
390])
```

Our inputs will consist of three time steps with two features per time step. The output will also consist of three time steps with one feature per time step.

Script 33:

```
1.  X = np.array(X).reshape(20, 3, 2)
2.  y = np.array(y).reshape(20, 3, 1)
```

Here is how the input looks.

Script 34:

```
1.  print(x)
```

You can see three time steps per input and two features per time step.

Output:

```
array([[[  6,    7],
         [ 12,   14],
         [ 18,   21]],

        [[ 24,   28],
         [ 30,   35],
         [ 36,   42]],

        [[ 42,   49],
         [ 48,   56],
         [ 54,   63]],

        [[ 60,   70],
         [ 66,   77],
         [ 72,   84]],

        [[ 78,   91],
         [ 84,   98],
         [ 90,  105]],

        [[ 96,  112],
         [102,  119],
         [108,  126]],

        [[114,  133],
         [120,  140],
         [126,  147]],

        [[132,  154],
         [138,  161],
         [144,  168]],

        [[150,  175],
         [156,  182],
         [162,  189]],
```

```
[[168, 196],
 [174, 203],
 [180, 210]],

[[186, 217],
 [192, 224],
 [198, 231]],

[[204, 238],
 [210, 245],
 [216, 252]],

[[222, 259],
 [228, 266],
 [234, 273]],

[[240, 280],
 [246, 287],
 [252, 294]],

[[258, 301],
 [264, 308],
 [270, 315]],

[[276, 322],
 [282, 329],
 [288, 336]],

[[294, 343],
 [300, 350],
 [306, 357]],

[[312, 364],
 [318, 371],
 [324, 378]],

[[330, 385],
 [336, 392],
 [342, 399]],
```

```
[[348, 406],
 [354, 413],
 [360, 420]]])
```

To solve many to many sequence problems, we use the encoder decoder model. The encoder is an LSTM which accepts the input sequence. The decoder decodes the input sequence, and a time distributed dense layer is used to produce the output. The repeat vector is used to connect the encoder with the decoder. We use a time distributed dense layer because though there are three time steps in the output, at one time, only one of the time steps will be predicted. Here is the code for our neural network model.

Script 35:

```
1.   from tensorflow.keras.layers import RepeatVector
2.   from tensorflow.keras.layers import TimeDistributed
3.
4.   input_layer = Input(shape = (3,2))
5.   lstm1 = LSTM(100, activation='relu')(input_layer)
6.   rv = RepeatVector(3)(lstm1)
7.   lstm2 = LSTM(100, activation='relu', return_
     sequences=True)(rv)
8.   output_layer = TimeDistributed(Dense(1))(lstm2)
9.   model = Model(input_layer, output_layer)
10.  model.compile(optimizer='adam', loss='mse')
```

The following script plots the architecture for our neural network.

Script 36:

```
1.   from tensorflow.keras.utils import plot_model
2.   plot_model(model, to_file='model_plot1.png', show_
     shapes=True, show_layer_names=True)
```

Output:

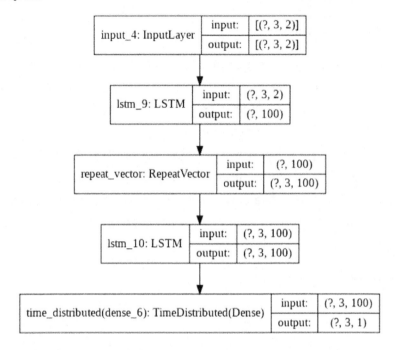

Finally, run the following script to train the model.

Script 37:

```
1.    model_history = model.fit(X, y, epochs=1000, verbose=1)
```

Output:

```
Epoch 996/1000
1/1 [==============================] - 0s 782us/step - loss:
0.0136
Epoch 997/1000
1/1 [==============================] - 0s 818us/step - loss:
0.0172
Epoch 998/1000
1/1 [==============================] - 0s 745us/step - loss:
0.0162
Epoch 999/1000
1/1 [==============================] - 0s 821us/step - loss:
0.0119
```

```
Epoch 1000/1000
1/1 [==============================] - 0s 730us/step - loss:
0.0105
```

The loss over number of epochs can be plotted via the following script.

Script 38:

```
1.  import matplotlib.pyplot as plt
2.
3.  plt.plot(model_history.history['loss'], label = 'loss')
4.  plt.legend(['train'], loc='top right')
```

Output:

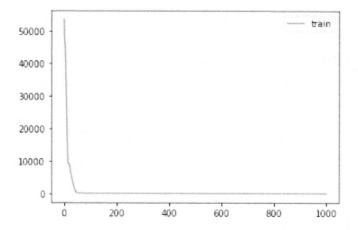

Finally, you can predict a new test point using the following script.

Script 39:

```
1.  X1 = [600, 606, 612]
2.  X2 = [700, 707, 714]
3.
4.  X_test = np.column_stack((X1, X2))
5.  X_test = X_test.reshape((1, 3, 2))
6.  y_pred = model.predict(X_test, verbose=0)
7.  print(y_pred)
```

Output:

```
[[[634.26917]
  [645.52606]
  [654.70337]]]
```

6.3. Predicting Future Stock Prices Via LSTM in Keras

Stock price prediction is perhaps one of the most common applications of many to one or many to many sequence problems.

In this section, we will predict the opening stock price of the Facebook company, using the opening stock price of the previous 60 days. The training set consists of the stock price data of Facebook from 1st January 2015 to 31st December 2019, i.e., 5 years. The dataset can be downloaded from this site: https://finance.yahoo.com/quote/FB/history?p=FB.

The test data will consist of the opening stock prices of the Facebook company for the month of January 2020. The training file fb_train.csv and the test file fb_test.csv are also available in the Datasets folder of the resources that accompany this book. Let's begin with the coding now.

6.3.1. Training the Stock Prediction Model

In this section, we will train our stock prediction model on the training set.

The following script imports the training file.

Script 40:

```
1.  import pandas as pd
2.  import numpy as np
3.  fb_complete_data = pd.read_csv("/content/fb_train.csv")
```

Running the following script will print the first five rows of the dataset.

Script 41:

```
1.  fb_complete_data.head()
```

Output:

	Date	Open	High	Low	Close	Adj Close	Volume
0	2015-01-02	78.580002	78.930000	77.699997	78.449997	78.449997	18177500
1	2015-01-05	77.980003	79.250000	76.860001	77.190002	77.190002	26452200
2	2015-01-06	77.230003	77.589996	75.360001	76.150002	76.150002	27399300
3	2015-01-07	76.760002	77.360001	75.820000	76.150002	76.150002	22045300
4	2015-01-08	76.739998	78.230003	76.080002	78.180000	78.180000	23961000

The output shows that our dataset consists of seven columns. However, in this section, we are only interested in the Open column. Therefore, we will select the Open column from the dataset. Run the following script to do so.

Script 42:

```
1.  fb_training_processed = fb_complete_data[['Open']].values
```

Next, we will scale our dataset.

Script 43:

```
1.  from sklearn.preprocessing import MinMaxScaler
2.  scaler = MinMaxScaler(feature_range = (0, 1))
3.
4.  fb_training_scaled = scaler.fit_transform(fb_training_
    processed)
```

If you check the total length of the dataset, you will see it has 1,257 records as shown below:

Script 44:

```
1.   len(fb_training_scaled)
```

Output:

```
1257
```

Before we move forward, we need to divide our data into features and labels. Our feature set will consist of 60 time steps of 1 feature. The feature set basically consists of the opening stock price of the past 60 days, while the label set will consist of the opening stock price of the 61st day. Based on the opening stock prices of the previous days, we will be predicting the opening stock price for the next day.

Script 45:

```
1.   fb_training_features= []
2.   fb_training_labels = []
3.   for i in range(60, len(fb_training_scaled)):
4.       fb_training_features.append(fb_training_scaled[i-60:i,
     0])
5.       fb_training_labels.append(fb_training_scaled[i, 0])
```

We need to convert our data into a Numpy array before we can use it as input with Keras. The following script does that:

Script 46:

```
1.   X_train = np.array(fb_training_features)
2.   y_train = np.array(fb_training_labels)
```

Let's print the shape of our dataset.

Script 47:

```
1.   print(X_train.shape)
2.   print(y_train.shape)
```

Output:

```
(1197, 60)
(1197,)
```

We need to reshape our input features into a three-dimensional format.

Script 48:

```
1.  X_train = np.reshape(X_train, (X_train.shape[0], X_train.
    shape[1], 1))
```

The following script creates our LSTM model. We have four LSTM layers with 100 nodes each. A dropouot layer follows each LSTM layer to avoid overfitting. The final dense layer has one node since the output is a single value.

Script 49:

```
1.  import numpy as np
2.  import matplotlib.pyplot as plt
3.  from tensorflow.keras.layers import Input, Activation,
    Dense, Flatten, Dropout,  Flatten, LSTM
4.  from tensorflow.keras.models import Model
```

Script 50:

```
1.  input_layer = Input(shape = (X_train.shape[1], 1))
2.  lstm1 = LSTM(100, activation='relu', return_
    sequences=True)(input_layer)
3.  do1 = Dropout(0.2)(lstm1)
4.  lstm2 = LSTM(100, activation='relu', return_
    sequences=True)(do1)
5.  do2 = Dropout(0.2)(lstm2)
6.  lstm3 = LSTM(100, activation='relu', return_
    sequences=True)(do2)
7.  do3 = Dropout(0.2)(lstm3)
8.  lstm4 = LSTM(100, activation='relu')(do3)
9.  do4 = Dropout(0.2)(lstm4)
10.
```

```
11.  output_layer = Dense(1)(do4)
12.  model = Model(input_layer, output_layer)
13.  model.compile(optimizer='adam', loss='mse')
```

Next, we need to convert the output y into a column vector.

Script 51:

```
1.   print(X_train.shape)
2.   print(y_train.shape)
3.   y_train= y_train.reshape(-1,1)
4.   print(y_train.shape)
```

Output:

```
(1197, 60, 1)
(1197,)
(1197, 1)
```

The following script trains our stock price prediction model on the training set.

Script 52:

```
1.   model_history = model.fit(X_train, y_train, epochs=100,
     verbose=1, batch_size = 32)
```

You can see the results for the last five epochs in the output.

Output:

```
Epoch 96/100
38/38 [==============================] - 11s 299ms/step -
loss: 0.0018
Epoch 97/100
38/38 [==============================] - 11s 294ms/step -
loss: 0.0019
Epoch 98/100
38/38 [==============================] - 11s 299ms/step -
loss: 0.0018
Epoch 99/100
38/38 [==============================] - 12s 304ms/step -
loss: 0.0018
```

```
Epoch 100/100
38/38 [==============================] - 11s 299ms/step -
loss: 0.0021
```

Our model has been trained. Next, we will test our stock prediction model on the test data.

6.3.2. Testing the Stock Prediction Model

The test data should also be converted into the right shape to test our stock prediction model. We will do that later. Let's first import the data, and then remove all the columns from the test data except the **Open** column.

Script 53:

```
1.  fb_testing_complete_data = pd.read_csv("/content/fb_test.
    csv")
2.  fb_testing_processed = fb_testing_complete_data[['Open']].
    values
```

Let's concatenate the training and test sets. We do this because to predict the first value in the test set, the input will be the data from the past 60 days, which is basically the data from the last 60 days in the training set.

Script 54:

```
1.  fb_all_data = pd.concat((fb_complete_data['Open'], fb_
    testing_complete_data['Open']), axis=0)
```

The following script creates our final input feature set.

Script 55:

```
1.  test_inputs = fb_all_data [len(fb_all_data ) - len(fb_
    testing_complete_data) - 60:].values
2.  print(test_inputs.shape)
```

You can see that the length of the input data is 80. Here, the first 60 records are the last 60 records from the training data, and the last 20 records are the 20 records from the test file.

Output:

```
(80,)
```

We need to scale our data and convert it into a column vector.

Script 56:

```
1.  test_inputs = test_inputs.reshape(-1,1)
2.  test_inputs = scaler.transform(test_inputs)
3.  print(test_inputs.shape)
```

Output:

```
(80, 1)
```

As with the training data, we need to divide our input data into features and labels. Here is the script that does that.

Script 57:

```
1.  fb_test_features = []
2.  for i in range(60, 80):
3.      fb_test_features.append(test_inputs[i-60:i, 0])
```

Let's now print our feature set.

Script 58:

```
1.  X_test = np.array(fb_test_features)
2.  print(X_test.shape)
```

Output:

```
(20, 60)
```

Our feature set is currently 2-dimensional. But the LSTM algorithm in Keras except data is 3-dimensional. The following script converts our input features into a 3-dimensional shape.

Script 59:

```
1.  X_test = np.reshape(X_test, (X_test.shape[0], X_test.
    shape[1], 1))
2.  print(X_test.shape)
```

Output:

```
(20, 60, 1)
```

Now is the time to make predictions on the test set. The following script does that.

Script 60:

```
1.  y_pred = model.predict(X_test)
```

Since we scaled our input feature, to get the original output values, we need to apply the **inverse_transform()** method of the **scaler** object on the predicted output.

Script 61:

```
1.  y_pred = scaler.inverse_transform(y_pred)
```

Finally, to compare the predicted output with the actual stock price values, you can plot the two values via the following script:

Script 62:

```
1.  plt.figure(figsize=(8,6))
2.  plt.plot(fb_testing_processed, color='red', label='Actual
    Facenook Stock Price')
3.  plt.plot(y_pred , color='green', label='Predicted Face
    Stock Price')
4.  plt.title('Facebook Stock Prices')
5.  plt.xlabel('Date')
6.  plt.ylabel('Stock Price')
7.  plt.legend()
8.  plt.show()
```

Output:

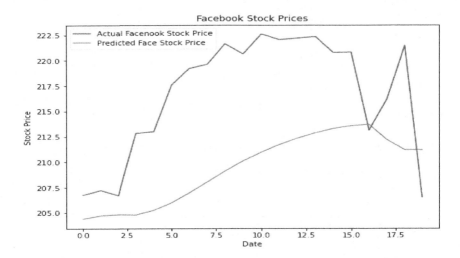

The output shows that our algorithm has been able to partially capture the trend of the future opening stock prices for Facebook data.

In the next chapter, you will see how to perform natural language processing with deep learning. We will use convolutional and recurrent neural networks for the sentiment classification tasks.

Exercise 6.1

Question 1:

The shape of the feature set passed to the LSTM's input layer should be:

1. Number of Records, Features, Time steps
2. Time steps, Features, Number of Records
3. Features, Time steps, Number of Records
4. Number of Records, Time steps, Features

Question 2:

To connect the encoder with a decoder layer in many to many sequence problems, which layer is used:

1. Time distributed
2. Repeat vector
3. Dense
4. Softmax

Question 3:

Image to text description is an example of:

1. One to One Sequence Problems
2. Many to One Sequence Problems
3. Many to Many Sequence Problems
4. One to Many Sequence Problems

Exercise 6.2

Using the Facebook training and testing data provided in the dataset, predict the closing stock price of the Facebook company for the next day.

7

Deep Learning for Natural Language Processing

7.1. Introduction

Humans communicate with each other in natural languages such as English, French, Spanish, etc. In order to communicate with computers, computer languages have been designed. The goal of natural language processing (NLP) is to communicate with computers in human languages. The advent of big data and high-performance computing has revitalized the interest in natural language processing.

Deep learning has several applications in natural language processing. Nowadays, deep learning is being used for various natural language applications such as text generation, text classification, topic modeling, text summarization, etc.

7.1.1. Applications of Natural Language Processing

Natural language processing has various applications. Some of these applications have been enlisted below:

1. **Text classification:**

   NLP techniques are used to automatically classify texts into different categories. For instance, you can classify text messages as ham or spam using NLP techniques. Text sentimental analysis is another application of NLP.

2. **Topic Modeling:**

   Topic modeling refers to assigning topics to various text documents. Topic modeling is an unsupervised deep learning task that various algorithms are trained on various unlabeled documents, and the documents having the same topics are grouped together.

3. **Text Translation**

   Deep learning techniques have outperformed all the traditional techniques for translating texts from one language to another.

4. **Text Summarization**

   Text Summarization refers to summarizing large texts into a smaller number of words. Deep learning techniques have been found quite useful for text translation too.

5. **Text Generation**

   Text Generation refers to generating text using image, text, or any other data type as input. Deep learning algorithms are commonly used for text generation tasks.

7.1.2. Preprocessing Tasks in NLP

Before you can actually use text data for performing several deep learning tasks, you need to preprocess text. The following are some of the most commonly used preprocessing tasks.

1. Tokenization

Tokenization refers to dividing a document into a list of individual words. You can use the **word_tokenize()** method from the NLTK library to tokenize text, as shown below:

Example:

```
1.    import nltk
2.    text = "Hello, this is a very useful book for deep
      learning"
3.    tokens = nltk.word_tokenize(text)
4.    print(tokens)
```

Output:

```
['Hello', ',', 'this', 'is', 'a', 'very', 'useful', 'book',
'for', 'deep', 'learning']
```

2. Stemming and Lemmatization

Stemming essentially means reducing a word to its stem form. For instance, the stem of the word computer, computed, and computing is **comput**. Here is an example of how you can perform stemming with the NLTK library.

Example:

```
1.    from nltk.stem import PorterStemmer
2.    words = ["Compute", "Computer", "Computing", "Computed",
      "Computes"]
3.    ps =PorterStemmer()
4.    for word in words :
5.        stem=ps.stem(word)
6.        print(stem)
```

Output:

```
comput
comput
comput
comput
comput
```

Lemmatization essentially means reducing a word to its root form, as found in the dictionary. Lemmatization is different from stemming. In stemming, a word is reduced to its root form even if the root has no meaning. On the other hand, in lemmatization, a word is reduced to its meaningful representation, as found in a dictionary. The following script shows how to perform lemmatization using the NLTK library.

Example:

```
1.  import nltk
2.  from nltk.stem import    WordNetLemmatizer
3.  wordnet_lemmatizer = WordNetLemmatizer()
4.  words = ["acts","acted", "smiles", "smile"]
5.
6.  for word in words :
7.      lemma = wordnet_lemmatizer.lemmatize(word)
8.      print(lemma)
```

Output:

```
act
acted
smile
smile
```

3. **Stop Word Removal**

Stop words are everyday words such as *a, is, am, it, he,* and *she.* Depending upon the task at hand, these words may or may not play any role while training the deep learning algorithms. Sometimes, stop words are removed altogether from the dataset. The following script shows how you can remove stop words from a dataset.

Example:

```
1.  from nltk.corpus import stopwords
2.  nltk.download('stopwords')
3.  from nltk.tokenize import word_tokenize
4.
5.  text = "Hello, this is a very useful book for deep
    learning"
6.  word_tokens = word_tokenize(text)
7.
8.  text_without_stopwords = [word for word in word_tokens if
    not word in stopwords.words()]
9.
10. print(" ".join(text_without_stopwords))
```

Output:

```
Hello , useful book deep learning
```

4. Parts of Speech Tagging

You often need to find parts of speech of the words in a sentence. With NLTK, you can easily find if a word is a verb, noun, pronoun, or any other part of speech. The following script shows how to do parts of speech tagging using NLTK.

Example:

```
1.  import nltk
2.  text = "Hello, this is a very useful book for deep
    learning"
3.  tokens = nltk.word_tokenize(text)
4.  nltk.pos_tag(tokens)
```

Output:

```
[('Hello', 'NNP'),
 (',', ','),
 ('this', 'DT'),
 ('is', 'VBZ'),
 ('a', 'DT'),
 ('very', 'RB'),
 ('useful', 'JJ'),
 ('book', 'NN'),
 ('for', 'IN'),
 ('deep', 'JJ'),
 ('learning', 'NN')]
```

5. Text Cleaning

Text cleaning refers to removing unwanted content from the text. For instance, you might want to remove all special characters and numbers from the text before feeding the text to a deep learning algorithm. You can use regex expressions to remove clean text. The following script imports re module and removes all the special characters and numbers from the text.

Example:

```
1.   import re
2.
3.   ## removenumbers and specialcharacters
4.   text = "Hello, mycellnumberis 12121121 and my email is:
     abc@xyz"
5.   cleaned_text = re.sub('[^a-zA-Z]', ' ', text)
6.   print(cleaned_text)
7.
8.   ## replace multiple spaces by a single space
9.   cleaned_text2  = re.sub(r'\s+', ' ', cleaned_text)
10.  print(cleaned_text2)
```

Output:

```
Hello  my cell number is            and my email is  abcxyz
Hello my cell number is and my email is abcxyz
```

Note: To know more about regex, take a look at this link:

https://www.w3schools.com/python/python_regex.asp

7.1.3. Steps in Building an NLP Application with Deep Learning

The following are the distinctive steps involved in developing an NLP application with a deep learning algorithm.

1. The first step is to import the text data into your application. You can either directly use flat files or import your text data into the Pandas dataframe. I prefer importing text to Pandas dataframe for preprocessing.

2. The second step is to preprocess text. Depending upon the task, preprocessing steps may involve cleaning text by removing numbers and special characters, tokenization, stemming, and parts of speech tagging.

3. The next step is to convert textual data into a numeric representation. There are various ways to do that, e.g., a bag of words approach, n-gram approach, word embeddings, etc. For deep learning, word embedding approaches are recommended. Word embedding approaches have been explained in the next section.

4. Once the text is converted to numbers, you can train your deep learning algorithms on the text. Depending upon the task, you can perform classification, regression, or clustering.

5. The outputs of deep learning algorithms are also numbers. In some cases, for instance, for text translation or text generation, you need to convert the predicted numeric output of deep learning algorithms back to text. Converting numeric data back to text depends upon the approach used to convert text to numeric data.

In this chapter, you will see how to use deep learning algorithms such as densely connected neural networks and convolutional neural networks to perform text classification and sentimental analysis.

The next section explains the word embedding process that is used to convert textual data to numeric data so that the data can be used to train machine learning algorithms.

7.2. Word Embeddings for Deep Learning

Deep learning algorithms are based on mathematics, and mathematics works with numbers. Therefore, in order to perform natural language processing with deep learning, you have to convert text to numbers. The simplest way to convert text to numbers is by using Word Embeddings. In this section, you will see how to perform Word Embeddings using the TensorFlow Keras library. So, let's begin without much ado.

As always, we will start by importing the required libraries:

Script 1:

```
1.  import pandas as pd
2.  import numpy as np
3.  import re
4.  import nltk
5.  from nltk.corpus import stopwords
6.
7.  from numpy import array
8.  from tensorflow.keras.preprocessing.text import one_hot
9.  from tensorflow.keras.preprocessing.sequence import pad_
    sequences
10. from tensorflow.keras.models import Sequential
11. from tensorflow.keras.layers import Activation, Dropout,
    Dense, Flatten, GlobalMaxPooling1D, Embedding, Conv1D,
    Input
12. from tensorflow.keras.models import Model
13. from sklearn.model_selection import train_test_split
14. from tensorflow.keras.preprocessing.text import Tokenizer
```

Next, we need to download various modules from NLTK (Natural language toolkit) library.

Script 2:

```
1.  import nltk
2.  nltk.download('stopwords')
3.  nltk.download('wordnet')
4.  nltk.download('punkt')
5.  nltk.download('averaged_perceptron_tagger')
```

Check out this link to study more about NLTK: https://www.nltk.org/

In the following script, we create a list of sentences. These are just fictional reviews about some movies. The first eight reviews are positive, while the last eight reviews are negative. We will use these reviews to explain word embeddings in this section.

Script 3:

```
1.   dataset = [
2.
3.
4.       'This movie is excellent',
5.       'I loved the movie, it was fantastic',
6.       'The film is brilliant, you should watch',
7.       'Wonderful movie',
8.       'one of the best films ever',
9.       'fantastic film to watch',
10.      'great movie',
11.      'Acting and direction is brilliant',
12.
13.
14.
15.      "poor acting",
16.      'horrible film',
17.      'pathetic acting',
18.      'The film is very boring',
19.      'I wasted my money',
20.      'I did not like the film',
21.      'not recommended',
22.      'it was a poor story'
23. ]
```

The following script defines the labels for our reviews. You can see that the first eight labels contain one (positive) while the last eight reviews contain 0 (negative).

Script 4:

```
1.   labels = np.array([1,1,1,1,1,1,1,1,0,0,0,0,0,0,0,0])
```

Firstly, we need to divide the sentences or reviews in our dataset into individual words. To do so, you can use the **Tokenizer** class from the **tensorflow.keras.preprocessing.text** module. The **fit_on_texts()** method of the **Tokenizer** class assigns an integer value to every unique word in our corpus.

Script 5:

```
1.   tokenizer = Tokenizer()
2.   tokenizer.fit_on_texts(dataset)
```

We need to find the total number of unique words in our dataset. We can do so using the following script:

Script 6:

```
1.   vocabulary_length = len(tokenizer.word_index) + 1
```

Next, we want to convert our text to numbers. The following script does that.

Script 7:

```
1.   integer_sentences = tokenizer.texts_to_sequences(dataset)
2.   print(integer_sentences)
```

Output:

```
[[14, 3, 4, 15], [5, 16, 1, 3, 7, 8, 9],
[1, 2, 4, 10, 17, 18, 11], [19, 3], [20, 21, 1, 22, 23, 24],
[9, 2, 25, 11], [26, 3], [6, 27, 28, 4, 10], [12, 6], [29, 2],
[30, 6], [1, 2, 4, 31, 32], [5, 33, 34, 35],
[5, 36, 13, 37, 1, 2], [13, 38], [7, 8, 39, 12, 40]]
```

Different sentences can have different lengths. For instance, from the above output, you can see that the first sentence has four words, while the second sentence has seven words. Neural networks in Keras expect input sentences to be of the same length. What we can do here is find the length of the longest sentence and then add zeros to the right of the sentences that are shorter than the longest sentence. This process is called padding. The following script performs padding on our dataset.

Script 8:

```
1.  from nltk.tokenize import word_tokenize
2.
3.  token_count = lambda sentence: len(word_
    tokenize(sentence))
4.  max_sentence = max(dataset, key = token_count)
5.  max_sentence_length = len(word_tokenize(max_sentence))
6.
7.  padded_reviews = pad_sequences(integer_sentences , max_
    sentence_length, padding='post')
8.
9.  print(padded_reviews)
```

Output:

```
[[14  3  4 15  0  0  0  0]
 [ 5 16  1  3  7  8  9  0]
 [ 1  2  4 10 17 18 11  0]
 [19  3  0  0  0  0  0  0]
 [20 21  1 22 23 24  0  0]
 [ 9  2 25 11  0  0  0  0]
 [26  3  0  0  0  0  0  0]
 [ 6 27 28  4 10  0  0  0]
 [12  6  0  0  0  0  0  0]
 [29  2  0  0  0  0  0  0]
 [30  6  0  0  0  0  0  0]
 [ 1  2  4 31 32  0  0  0]
 [ 5 33 34 35  0  0  0  0]
 [ 5 36 13 37  1  2  0  0]
 [13 38  0  0  0  0  0  0]
 [ 7  8 39 12 40  0  0  0]]
```

Now in the above output, you can see that all the sentences are of equal length, and zeros have been appended to the right of the sentences that are shorter in length than the longest sentence.

For word embeddings, you have two options. You can either train your own word embeddings, or you can use pretrained word embeddings. In pretrained word embeddings, for each word, you have pretrained vector representation. Glove and Stanford are the two most commonly used pretrained word embeddings. We will be using the Glove word embeddings in this chapter.

The Glove word embeddings are available at this link:

https://nlp.stanford.edu/projects/glove/

The link contains word embeddings of various sizes. We will be using 100-dimensional word embeddings. The word embedding file is also available in the datasets folder. The following script imports the Glove word embeddings into your application.

Script 9:

```
1.   from numpy import array
2.   from numpy import asarray
3.   from numpy import zeros
4.
5.   embedd_dict= dict()
6.   glove_embeddings = open('/gdrive/My Drive/datasets/
     glove.6B.100d.txt', encoding="utf8")
```

Next, we will design a dictionary where the keys will be the names of the words, and the values will be the corresponding word embedding vectors.

Script 10:

```
1.   for embeddings in glove_embeddings:
2.       embedding_tokens = embeddings.split()
3.       emb_word = embedding_tokens [0]
4.       emb_vector = asarray(  embedding_tokens[1:],
     dtype='float32')
5.       embedd_dict [emb_word] = emb_vector
6.
7.   glove_embeddings.close()
```

Finally, we will create a matrix where the row numbers of the matrix correspond to the index numbers for all the unique words in our dataset and columns contain the corresponding word embedding matrix from the glove word embedding.

Script 11:

```
1.    embedd_mat= zeros((vocabulary_length, 100))
2.    for word, index in tokenizer.word_index.items():
3.        embedding_vector = embedd_dict.get(word)
4.        if embedding_vector is not None:
5.            embedd_mat[index] = embedding_vector
```

Let's see the shape of our embedding matrix.

Script 12:

```
1.    embedd_mat.shape
```

Since there are 41 unique words in our corpus, the number of rows of the matrix is 41, and since each word is represented by a 100-dimensional vector, the column size is 100 as shown below:

Output:

```
(41, 100)
```

We have created our embedding matrix that contains Glove word embeddings for the words in our corpus. Now, we can train our Neural Network Model in Keras. If you want to use word embeddings with your neural network model, you have to use **Embedding()** layer after the input layer and before any other layer in the neural network. The first parameter to the embedding layer is your vocabulary size, and the second parameter is the number of dimensions of the output vector. Also, the embedding matrix is passed to the **weights** parameter. Finally, you have to set the **trainable** attribute to **False**. The shape of the input layer will be the maximum sentence length. If you want to connect the output of the **Embedding** layer directly to a **Dense** layer, you have to flatten the result of the Embedding layer.

In the following script, we create a simple model with one input layer, embedding layer, flattening layer, and one densely connected layer.

Script 13:

```
1.  embedding_inputs = Input(shape=(max_sentence_length))
2.  embedding_layer = Embedding(vocabulary_length, 100,
    weights=[embedd_mat], trainable=False)(embedding_inputs)
3.  flatten_layer = Flatten()(embedding_layer)
4.  output_layer = Dense(1, activation='sigmoid')(flatten_
    layer)
5.  model = Model(inputs=embedding_inputs, outputs=output_
    layer)
```

The following script compiles the model and prints its summary.

Script 14:

```
1.  model.compile(optimizer='adam', loss='binary_
    crossentropy', metrics=['acc'])
2.  print(model.summary())
```

Output:

```
Model: "model"

Layer (type)                  Output Shape              Param #
=================================================================
input_1 (InputLayer)          [(None, 8)]                  0

embedding (Embedding)         (None, 8, 100)            4100

flatten (Flatten)             (None, 800)                  0

dense (Dense)                 (None, 1)                  801
=================================================================
Total params: 4,901
Trainable params: 801
Non-trainable params: 4,100

None
```

Finally, the following script trains the model and then evaluates it on the dataset itself. You can see that the process of training a model is similar to any other neural network.

Script 15:

```
1.  model.fit(padded_reviews, labels, epochs=100, verbose=1)
2.  loss, accuracy = model.evaluate(padded_reviews, labels,
    verbose=0)
3.
4.  print('Accuracy: %f' % (accuracy*100))
```

Here is the output of the last five epochs.

Output:

```
Epoch 96/100
1/1 [==============================] - 0s 2ms/step - loss:
0.1339 - acc: 1.0000
Epoch 97/100
1/1 [==============================] - 0s 3ms/step - loss:
0.1322 - acc: 1.0000
Epoch 98/100
1/1 [==============================] - 0s 3ms/step - loss:
0.1307 - acc: 1.0000
Epoch 99/100
1/1 [==============================] - 0s 2ms/step - loss:
0.1291 - acc: 1.0000
Epoch 100/100
1/1 [==============================] - 0s 2ms/step - loss:
0.1276 - acc: 1.0000
Accuracy: 100.000000
```

The result shows that an accuracy of 100 percent is achieved on the dataset after 100 epochs, which is impressive.

In the next section, we will see a more real-world example of text classification when we perform sentimental analysis of public tweets about a certain airline.

7.3. Sentiment Analysis with DNN

In this section, we will be performing the text sentimental analysis of public tweets regarding different US airlines. Text sentimental analysis refers to finding sentiment or opinion from a piece of text, which can be a review, a tweet, a blog, or any other piece of text.

The dataset we use for this section is freely available at this link:

https://raw.githubusercontent.com/kolaveridi/kaggle-Twitter-US-Airline-Sentiment-/master/Tweets.csv

In addition, the data is also available in the dataset folder that accompanies this book.

So, let's begin without much ado. We start by importing the required libraries.

Script 16:

```
1.  import pandas as pd
2.  import numpy as np
3.  import re
4.  import nltk
5.  from nltk.corpus import stopwords
6.
7.  from numpy import array
8.  from tensorflow.keras.preprocessing.text import one_hot
9.  from tensorflow.keras.preprocessing.sequence import pad_
    sequences
10. from tensorflow.keras.models import Sequential
11. from tensorflow.keras.layers import Activation, LSTM,
    Dropout, Dense, Flatten, Input,  Embedding, Conv1D, Input
12. from tensorflow.keras.models import Model
13. from sklearn.model_selection import train_test_split
14. from tensorflow.keras.preprocessing.text import Tokenizer
```

The following script imports the dataset and displays a part of dataset header:

Script 17:

```
1.  airline_data = pd.read_csv("/gdrive/My Drive/datasets/
    airline_review.csv")
2.  airline_data.head()
```

Output:

airline_sentiment	airline_sentiment_confidence	negativereason	negativereason_confidence	airline	airline_sentiment_gold	name	negativereason_gold	retweet_count	text
neutral	1.0000	NaN	NaN	Virgin America	NaN	cairdio	NaN	0	@VirginAmerica What @dhepburn said
positive	0.3486	NaN	0.0000	Virgin America	NaN	jnardino	NaN	0	@VirginAmerica plus you've added commercials t
neutral	0.6837	NaN	NaN	Virgin America	NaN	yvonnalynn	NaN	0	@VirginAmerica I didn't today Must mean I n
negative	1.0000	Bad Flight	0.7033	Virgin America	NaN	jnardino	NaN	0	@VirginAmerica it's really aggressive to blast
negative	1.0000	Can't Tell	1.0000	Virgin America	NaN	jnardino	NaN	0	@VirginAmerica and it's a really big bad thing

The airline_sentiment column contains the sentiment of tweets, and the text column contains texts of tweets.

Let's see the number of positive, negative, and neutral tweets.

Script 18:

```
1.  airline_data.airline_sentiment.value_counts()
```

Output:

```
negative    9178
neutral     3099
positive    2363
Name: airline_sentiment, dtype: int64
```

The output shows that majority of tweets are negative.

Let's divide the data into feature and label set.

Script 19:

```
1.  X = airline_data["text"]
2.
3.  y = pd.get_dummies(airline_data.airline_sentiment,
    prefix='sent').values
```

Let's see the shape of the outputs.

Script 20:

```
1.  y.shape
```

Output:

```
(14640, 3)
```

Since there are three possible labels, the output contains three columns.

Let's define a function that cleans the text.

Script 21:

```
1.   def clean_text(doc):
2.
3.       document = remove_tags(doc)
4.
5.       document = re.sub('[^a-zA-Z]', ' ', document)
6.
7.       document = re.sub(r"\s+[a-zA-Z]\s+", ' ', document)
8.
9.       document = re.sub(r'\s+', ' ', document)
10.
11.      return document
```

If you have text that contains HTML contents, you can use the following function to remove HTML tags from text.

Script 22:

```
1.   TAG_RE = re.compile(r'<[^>]+>')
2.
3.   def remove_tags(document):
4.       return TAG_RE.sub('', document)
```

Next, we define a loop that cleans all the tweets.

Script 23:

```
1.   X_sentences = []
2.   reviews = list(X)
3.   for rev in reviews:
4.       X_sentences.append(clean_text(rev))
```

Finally, we divide our dataset into the training and test set.

Script 24:

```
1.  X_train, X_test, y_train, y_test = train_test_split(X_
    sentences, y, test_size=0.20, random_state=42)
```

From here on, the script will be similar to section 7.2. We will perform word embedding on our text tweets.

The following script tokenizes the text and then converts text to integers.

Script 25:

```
1.  tokenizer = Tokenizer(num_words=5000)
2.  tokenizer.fit_on_texts(X_train)
3.
4.  X_train = tokenizer.texts_to_sequences(X_train)
5.  X_test = tokenizer.texts_to_sequences(X_test)
```

The following script performs post padding of the tweets that are smaller than 100 characters, i.e., the maximum sentence length.

Script 26:

```
1.  vocab_size = len(tokenizer.word_index) + 1
2.
3.  maxlen = 100
4.
5.  X_train = pad_sequences(X_train, padding='post',
    maxlen=maxlen)
6.  X_test = pad_sequences(X_test, padding='post',
    maxlen=maxlen)
```

Next, we need to import the Glove word embeddings.

Script 27:

```
1.  from numpy import array
2.  from numpy import asarray
3.  from numpy import zeros
4.  embedd_dict= dict()
5.  glove_embeddings = open('/gdrive/My Drive/datasets/
    glove.6B.100d.txt', encoding="utf8")
```

The following script creates word embedding dictionary.

Script 28:

```
1.  for embeddings in glove_embeddings:
2.      embedding_tokens = embeddings.split()
3.      emb_word = embedding_tokens [0]
4.      emb_vector = asarray(   embedding_tokens[1:],
    dtype='float32')
5.      embedd_dict [emb_word] = emb_vector
6.
7.  glove_embeddings.close()
```

To create the embedding matrix, you can execute the following script.

Script 29:

```
1.  embedd_mat= zeros((vocab_size, 100))
2.  for word, index in tokenizer.word_index.items():
3.      embedding_vector = embedd_dict.get(word)
4.      if embedding_vector is not None:
5.          embedd_mat[index] = embedding_vector
```

The shape of the embedding matrix is as follows.

Script 30:

```
1.  embedd_mat.shape
```

Output:

```
(12085, 100)
```

Our embedding matrix contains 12,085 words, and one word is represented by a 100-dimensional vector.

The following script creates our DNN network.

Script 31:

```
1.  embedding_inputs = Input(shape=(maxlen))
2.  embedding_layer = Embedding(vocab_size, 100,
    weights=[embedd_mat], trainable=False)(embedding_inputs )
3.  flatten_layer = Flatten()(embedding_layer)
4.
5.  dense1 = Dense(512, activation='relu')(flatten_layer)
6.  do1 = Dropout(0.3)(dense1)
7.
8.  dense2 = Dense(512, activation='relu')(do1)
9.  do2 = Dropout(0.3)(dense2)
10.
11. dense3 = Dense(512, activation='relu')(do2)
12. do3 = Dropout(0.3)(dense3)
13.
14. output_layer = Dense(y_train.shape[1],
    activation='softmax')(do3)
15. model = Model(embedding_inputs, output_layer)
16.
17. model.compile(optimizer='adam', loss='categorical_
    crossentropy', metrics=['accuracy'])
```

To view the model architecture, run the following script.

Script 32:

```
1.  from tensorflow.keras.utils import plot_model
2.  plot_model(model, to_file='model_plot1.png', show_
    shapes=True, show_layer_names=True)
```

Output:

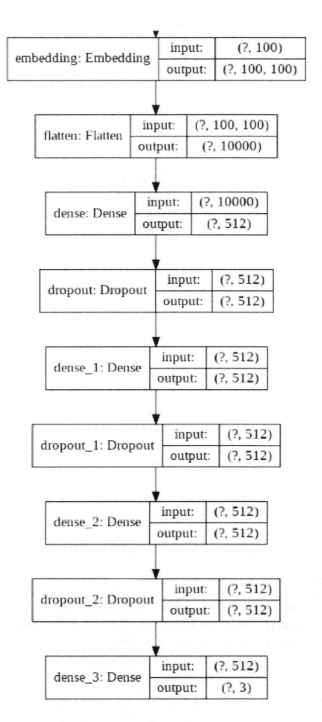

Finally, execute the following script to train the model.

Script 33:

```
1.   history = model.fit(X_train, y_train, batch_size= 64,
     epochs=10, verbose=1, validation_split=0.2)
2.
3.   score = model.evaluate(X_test, y_test, verbose=1)
```

Output:

```
Epoch 1/10
147/147 [==============================] - 8s 55ms/step -
loss: 0.7931 - accuracy: 0.6741 - val_loss: 0.6988 - val_
accuracy: 0.7153
Epoch 2/10
147/147 [==============================] - 8s 54ms/step -
loss: 0.6393 - accuracy: 0.7423 - val_loss: 0.6749 - val_
accuracy: 0.7354
Epoch 3/10
147/147 [==============================] - 8s 54ms/step -
loss: 0.5545 - accuracy: 0.7766 - val_loss: 0.6577 - val_
accuracy: 0.7375
Epoch 4/10
147/147 [==============================] - 8s 54ms/step -
loss: 0.4669 - accuracy: 0.8176 - val_loss: 0.6873 - val_
accuracy: 0.7431
Epoch 5/10
147/147 [==============================] - 8s 54ms/step -
loss: 0.3946 - accuracy: 0.8480 - val_loss: 0.7632 - val_
accuracy: 0.7153
Epoch 6/10
147/147 [==============================] - 8s 54ms/step -
loss: 0.3219 - accuracy: 0.8763 - val_loss: 0.7930 - val_
accuracy: 0.7341
Epoch 7/10
147/147 [==============================] - 8s 54ms/step -
loss: 0.2524 - accuracy: 0.9012 - val_loss: 1.0018 - val_
accuracy: 0.7200
```

```
Epoch 8/10
147/147 [==============================] - 8s 53ms/step -
loss: 0.2182 - accuracy: 0.9225 - val_loss: 0.9693 - val_
accuracy: 0.7162
Epoch 9/10
147/147 [==============================] - 8s 54ms/step -
loss: 0.1870 - accuracy: 0.9314 - val_loss: 1.0810 - val_
accuracy: 0.7358
Epoch 10/10
147/147 [==============================] - 8s 54ms/step -
loss: 0.1663 - accuracy: 0.9389 - val_loss: 1.1824 - val_
accuracy: 0.7315
92/92 [==============================] - 1s 12ms/step - loss:
1.0841 - accuracy: 0.7408
```

At the end of the 10th epoch, we achieve an accuracy of 74.08 percent on the training set.

The following script prints the loss and accuracy on the test set.

Script 34:

```
1.  print(score[0])
2.  print(score[1])
```

Output:

```
1.084073543548584
0.7407786846160889
```

7.4. Sentiment Analysis with CNN

In this section, we will use a convolutional neural network to perform sentimental analysis of the IMDB movie reviews. The dataset for this section is available by the name "IMDB Dataset.csv" in the resources folder that comes with this book.

We begin with importing the libraries we need.

Script 35:

```
1.  import pandas as pd
2.  import numpy as np
3.  import re
4.  import nltk
5.  from nltk.corpus import stopwords
6.
7.  from numpy import array
8.  from tensorflow.keras.preprocessing.text import one_hot
9.  from tensorflow.keras.preprocessing.sequence import pad_
    sequences
10. from tensorflow.keras.models import Sequential
11. from tensorflow.keras.layers import Activation, LSTM,
    Dropout, Dense, Flatten, Input,  Embedding, Conv1D, Input
12. from tensorflow.keras.models import Model
13. from sklearn.model_selection import train_test_split
14. from tensorflow.keras.preprocessing.text import Tokenizer
```

The following script imports the dataset.

Script 36:

```
1.  imdb_data= pd.read_csv("/gdrive/My Drive/datasets/IMDB
    Dataset.csv")
2.
3.  imdb_data.head()
```

Output:

	review	sentiment
0	One of the other reviewers has mentioned that ...	positive
1	A wonderful little production. The...	positive
2	I thought this was a wonderful way to spend ti...	positive
3	Basically there's a family where a little boy ...	negative
4	Petter Mattei's "Love in the Time of Money" is...	positive

The review column contains the text review, while the sentiment column contains the sentiment of the review. Let's see how many unique sentiments we have in our dataset.

Script 37:

```
1.   imdb_data.sentiment.value_counts()
```

Output:

```
positive    25000
negative    25000
Name: sentiment, dtype: int64
```

The output shows that we have 25,000 positive and 25,000 negative reviews in our dataset.

The following script divides the data into features and label set.

Script 38:

```
1.   X = imdb_data["review"]
2.
3.   y = pd.get_dummies(imdb_data.sentiment, prefix='sent',
     drop_first=True).values
```

Next, we define **clean_text()** function which cleans our text reviews from punctuations and special characters.

Script 39:

```
1.   def clean_text(doc):
2.
3.       document = remove_tags(doc)
4.
5.       document = re.sub('[^a-zA-Z]', ' ', document)
6.
7.       document = re.sub(r"\s+[a-zA-Z]\s+", ' ', document)
8.
9.       document = re.sub(r'\s+', ' ', document)
10.
11.      return document
```

If you have text that contains HTML contents, you can use the following function to remove HTML tags from text.

Script 40:

```
1.   TAG_RE = re.compile(r'<[^>]+>')
2.
3.   def remove_tags(document):
4.       return TAG_RE.sub('', document)
```

Next, we define a loop that cleans all the tweets.

Script 41:

```
1.   X_sentences = []
2.   reviews = list(X)
3.   for rev in reviews:
4.       X_sentences.append(clean_text(rev))
```

Finally, we divide our dataset into the training and test sets.

Script 42:

```
1.   X_train, X_test, y_train, y_test = train_test_split(X_
     sentences, y, test_size=0.20, random_state=42)
```

From here on, the script will be similar to section 7.2. We will perform word embedding on our text reviews.

The following script tokenizes the text and then converts text to integers.

Script 43:

```
1.   tokenizer = Tokenizer(num_words=5000)
2.   tokenizer.fit_on_texts(X_train)
3.
4.   X_train = tokenizer.texts_to_sequences(X_train)
5.   X_test = tokenizer.texts_to_sequences(X_test)
```

The following script performs post padding of the reviews that are smaller than 100 characters, i.e., the maximum sentence length.

Script 44:

```
1.   vocab_size = len(tokenizer.word_index) + 1
2.
3.   maxlen = 100
4.
5.   X_train = pad_sequences(X_train, padding='post',
     maxlen=maxlen)
6.   X_test = pad_sequences(X_test, padding='post',
     maxlen=maxlen)
```

Next, we need to import the Glove word embeddings.

Script 45:

```
1.   from numpy import array
2.   from numpy import asarray
3.   from numpy import zeros
4.
5.   embedd_dict= dict()
6.   glove_embeddings = open('/gdrive/My Drive/datasets/
     glove.6B.100d.txt', encoding="utf8")
```

The following script creates a word embedding dictionary.

Script 46:

```
1.   for embeddings in glove_embeddings:
2.       embedding_tokens = embeddings.split()
3.       emb_word = embedding_tokens [0]
4.       emb_vector = asarray(   embedding_tokens[1:],
     dtype='float32')
5.       embedd_dict [emb_word] = emb_vector
6.
7.   glove_embeddings.close()
```

To create the embedding matrix, you can execute the following script.

Script 47:

```
1.   embedd_mat= zeros((vocab_size, 100))
2.   for word, index in tokenizer.word_index.items():
3.       embedding_vector = embedd_dict.get(word)
4.       if embedding_vector is not None:
5.           embedd_mat[index] = embedding_vector
```

Finally, the following script creates our CNN model for sentiment classification. The model has an input layer, an embedding layer, two convolutional layers, one flat layer, and two dense layers. Also, drop out has been added after flatten and dense layers to avoid overfitting.

Script 48:

```
1.   embedding_inputs = Input(shape=(maxlen))
2.   embedding_layer = Embedding(vocab_size, 100,
     weights=[embedd_mat], trainable=False)(embedding_inputs )
3.   conv1 = Conv1D(128, 3, strides = 2, activation= 'relu')
     (embedding_layer)
4.   conv2 = Conv1D(64, 3, strides = 2, activation= 'relu')
     (conv1)
5.   flat1 = Flatten()(conv2)
6.   drop1 = Dropout(0.2)(flat1)
7.   dense1 = Dense(512, activation = 'relu')(drop1)
8.   drop2  = Dropout(0.2)(dense1)
9.   output_layer = Dense(1, activation= 'sigmoid')(drop2)
10.
11.  model = Model(embedding_inputs, output_layer )
12.
13.  model.compile(optimizer='adam', loss='binary_
     crossentropy', metrics=['accuracy'])
```

The following script prints the CNN architecture that we are using for sentiment classification.

Script 49:

```
1.   from tensorflow.keras.utils import plot_model
2.   plot_model(model, to_file='model_plot1.png', show_
     shapes=True, show_layer_names=True)
```

Output:

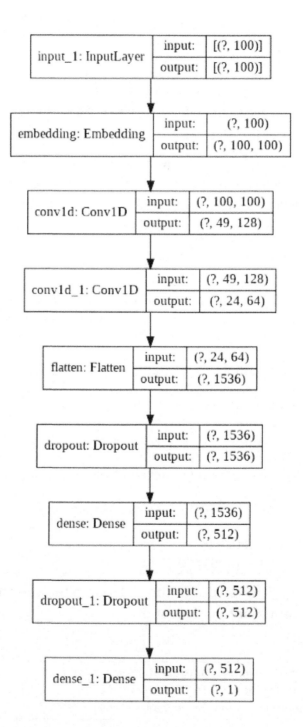

Finally, to train the model, execute the following script:

Script 50:

```
1.   history = model.fit(X_train, y_train, batch_size= 64,
     epochs=10, verbose=1, validation_split=0.2)
2.
3.   score = model.evaluate(X_test, y_test, verbose=1)
```

Output:

```
Epoch 1/10
500/500 [==============================] - 19s 37ms/step
- loss: 0.5289 - accuracy: 0.7250 - val_loss: 0.4257 - val_
accuracy: 0.8040
Epoch 2/10
500/500 [==============================] - 19s 37ms/step
- loss: 0.4055 - accuracy: 0.8146 - val_loss: 0.3895 - val_
accuracy: 0.8164
Epoch 3/10
500/500 [==============================] - 18s 37ms/step
- loss: 0.3660 - accuracy: 0.8346 - val_loss: 0.3856 - val_
accuracy: 0.8250
Epoch 4/10
500/500 [==============================] - 19s 38ms/step
- loss: 0.3135 - accuracy: 0.8631 - val_loss: 0.3936 - val_
accuracy: 0.8267
Epoch 5/10
500/500 [==============================] - 19s 39ms/step
- loss: 0.2682 - accuracy: 0.8841 - val_loss: 0.4436 - val_
accuracy: 0.8109
Epoch 6/10
500/500 [==============================] - 19s 39ms/step
- loss: 0.2238 - accuracy: 0.9066 - val_loss: 0.4731 - val_
accuracy: 0.8177
Epoch 7/10
500/500 [==============================] - 19s 38ms/step
- loss: 0.1810 - accuracy: 0.9257 - val_loss: 0.4826 - val_
accuracy: 0.8154
```

```
Epoch 8/10
500/500 [==============================] - 19s 38ms/step
- loss: 0.1494 - accuracy: 0.9402 - val_loss: 0.5777 - val_
accuracy: 0.7960
Epoch 9/10
500/500 [==============================] - 19s 38ms/step
- loss: 0.1180 - accuracy: 0.9534 - val_loss: 0.5960 - val_
accuracy: 0.8106
Epoch 10/10
500/500 [==============================] - 19s 38ms/step
- loss: 0.0979 - accuracy: 0.9623 - val_loss: 0.6725 - val_
accuracy: 0.8056
313/313 [==============================] - 2s 7ms/step - loss:
0.6692 - accuracy: 0.8042
```

After 10 epochs, we achieve an accuracy of 80.42percent on the training set.

To see the loss and accuracy on the test set, execute the following script:

Script 51:

```
1.  print(score[0])
2.  print(score[1])
```

Output:

```
0.6691895723342896
0.8041999936103821
```

On the test set, our model achieves an accuracy of 80.41 percent, which is almost similar to the training accuracy, i.e., 80.42 percent, which shows that our model is not overfitting.

This chapter showed how to perform natural language processing via deep learning. In the next chapter, you will study autoencoder, which is an unsupervised algorithm for deep learning.

Exercise 7.1

Question 1

Which of the following is not a pre-trained word embeddings?

1. Glove

2. Stanford

3. Peeking

4. All of the above

Question 2

What should be the first argument to the Keras Embedding Layer?

1. The input vector dimensions

2. The output vector dimensions

3. The word embedding size

4. The vocabulary size

Question 3

Which layer will you need to use if you want to directly connect the Embedding Layer with a Dense Layer?

1. LSTM layer with return_sequence set to False

2. CNN layer with max pooling

3. Flatten layer

4. None of the Above

Exercise 7.2

Using the IMDB dataset that we used for sentiment classification in section 7.4, perform sentiment classification using an RNN.

See if you can get better results with RNN as compared to the results in section 7.4.

Unsupervised Learning with Autoencoders

Till now, in this book, we have been focusing on supervised deep learning algorithms. In a supervised deep learning algorithm, the output label is given. The task of a supervised deep learning algorithm is to find relationships between input features and the output labels.

In unsupervised machine learning, however, the output label is not given. Raw data, without the output labels, is given to an unsupervised deep learning algorithm. The algorithm then finds the pattern between the data.

In this book, you will study Autoencoder, which is one of the most commonly used unsupervised deep learning algorithms.

8.1. What is an Autoencoder?

An autoencoder is an unsupervised deep learning algorithm commonly used for dimensionality reduction, image compression and reconstruction, and image denoising and anomaly detection.

There are various ways to implement an autoencoder. One of the ways is to use neural networks. The following figure shows the simplest autoencoder with an input layer, one hidden dense layer, and an output layer.

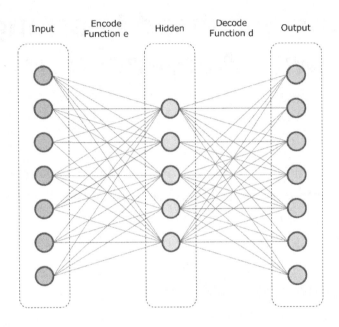

The above architecture is very similar to any densely connected neural network with one layer. The only difference here is that the number of nodes or neurons in the input layer is equal to the output layer. This is because the input and outputs to an autoencoder are the same.

The autoencoder has two main components: an encoder and a decoder. The role of the encoder is to encode input features into lower dimensional layers. The role of the decoder is to convert lower dimensional features back into the original inputs.

Let's see another example of an autoencoder with multiple hidden layers. In the following image, there is an input layer, two encoding layers, a hidden layer, and two decoding layers. The first encoding layer encodes six input features into three features, and the second encoding layer encodes three features in two nodes in the hidden layer. The input to the first decoder layer is the hidden layer. The first decoder layer converts two features back to three 3, and the second decoder layer converts three features back to six, which is the size of the inputs.

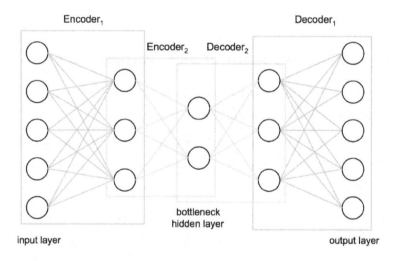

The hidden or bottleneck layer actually contains the reduced dimensions, which can represent a compressed image, or principal components, etc., depending upon the task. The inputs and outputs are the same. The weights of the encoding and hidden layers are calculated using the gradient descent function that you have already studied in chapters 2 and 3.

8.1.1. Characteristics of Autoencoders

There are three main characteristics of autoencoders:

1. Since autoencoding is a dimensionality reduction or compression algorithm, it depends upon the data it

is trained on. It can only compress or decompress the type of data on which the autoencoder is trained.

2. Compression algorithms try to encode higher dimensional data into lower dimensions. Hence, some of the information loss occurs. This is why autoencoders are called lossy algorithms.

3. Autoencoders automatically learn from data using forward propagation, backpropagation, and gradient descent algorithms.

8.1.2. Applications of Autoencoders

Autoencoders have various applications. Some of these applications are as follows:

1. Autoencoders are commonly used for dimensionality reduction in case if you have a huge number of features in your dataset.

2. Autoencoders are used for image processing tasks such as image compression, image denoising, image reconstruction, etc.

3. Autoencoders are also commonly used for developing recommendation systems.

4. Autoencoders are employed to solve sequence to sequence problems too.

5. Autoencoders are also used for clustering tasks such as anomaly detection.

In the following sections, you will see two applications of autoencoders: image compression and reconstruction, and anomaly detection.

8.2. Autoencoders for Image Compression and Reconstruction

Autoencoders are commonly used for image compression and reconstruction tasks. In this section, you will build a very simple autoencoder with one encoding and one decoding layer. The autoencoder you are going to build will perform the task of image compression and reconstruction. The encoding layer will be used to compress the image, while the decoding layer will be used to reconstruct the image from its compressed form.

You will be using the MNIST dataset that comes prebuilt with Keras and contains images of handwritten digits. The task will be to compress the handwritten image using an encoder and then reconstruct the image from its compressed form using a decoder, as shown in the following figure:

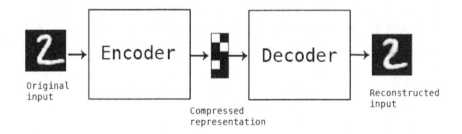

Note: The above image is taken from the Keras official blog.

To create our autoencoder, we will be following an example at Keras official blog.

Let's begin without much ado.

As a first step, we will import the required libraries:

Script 1:

```
1.  import pandas as pd
2.  import numpy as np
3.  import re
4.
5.  from numpy import array
6.  from tensorflow.keras.preprocessing.text import one_hot
7.
8.  from tensorflow.keras.models import Sequential
9.  from tensorflow.keras.layers import Activation, LSTM,
    Dropout, Dense, Flatten, Input, Embedding, Conv1D, Input
10. from tensorflow.keras.models import Model
11. from sklearn.model_selection import train_test_split
12. from tensorflow.keras import regularizers
13. from sklearn.metrics import recall_score, classification_
    report, auc, roc_curve, accuracy_score
```

The following script imports the dataset. You can see from the following script that we are only downloading the training and test images; we are not downloading the corresponding labels. This is because the input and output to the autoencoder in our case will be the same, i.e., training and testing images. Also the script prints the shape of the images.

Script 2:

```
1.  from keras.datasets import mnist
2.  import numpy as np
3.  (train_images, _), (test_images, _) = mnist.load_data()
4.  print (train_images.shape)
5.  print (test_images.shape)
```

The output shows that we have 60,000 two-dimensional images of shapes 28 x 28, and 10,000 test images of the same dimensions.

Output:

```
Using TensorFlow backend.
Downloading data from https://s3.amazonaws.com/img-datasets/
mnist.npz
11493376/11490434 [==============================] - 2s 0us/
step
(60000, 28, 28)
(10000, 28, 28)
```

Since we will only be using dense layers, we will reshape our images so that they become one-dimensional images of 28 x 28 = 784 pixels or input features. However, before that, we will normalize the images by dividing all image pixels by 255. Since we have greyscale images, therefore, the value of each pixel will be between 0 to 255. Hence, we can normalize images by dividing the image pixels by 255.

Script 3:

```
1.  train_images = train_images.astype('float32') / 255.
2.  test_images = test_images.astype('float32') / 255.
3.
4.  train_images = train_images.reshape((len(train_images),
    np.prod(train_images.shape[1:])))
5.
6.  test_images = test_images.reshape((len(test_images),
    np.prod(test_images.shape[1:])))
7.
8.  print (train_images.shape)
9.  print (test_images.shape)
```

Output:

```
60000, 784)
(10000, 784)
```

Now, we are ready to create our autoencoder, as shown in the following script. In the following script, we have one input feature layer with 784 input features. The only encoding layer encodes the input image to 32 dimensions. The final decoding layer, which is also the output layer, converts the compressed image back to its original size.

Script 4:

```
1.   from keras.layers import Input, Dense
2.   from keras.models import Model
3.
4.   encoding_dim = 32
5.
6.   # the input layer with 784 features
7.   input_layer = Input(shape=(784,))
8.   # the only hidden layer or the encoded layer with 32
     dimensions
9.   encoder_layer1 = Dense(encoding_dim, activation='relu')
     (input_layer)
10.  # the decoded layer with again 784 features
11.  decoder_layer1 = Dense(784, activation='sigmoid')(encoder_
     layer1)
12.
13.  # this model maps an input to its reconstruction
14.  autoencoder = Model(input_layer, decoder_layer1)
15.  autoencoder.summary()
```

The output shows the model summary, which clearly shows that we have 784 dimensions in the input, 32 dimensions in the hidden layer, and again 784 dimensions in the output layer.

Output:

```
Model: "model_1"

Layer (type)                  Output Shape              Param #
=================================================================
input_1 (InputLayer)          (None, 784)               0

dense_1 (Dense)               (None, 32)                25120

dense_2 (Dense)               (None, 784)               25872
=================================================================
Total params: 50,992
Trainable params: 50,992
Non-trainable params: 0
```

Next, we will create our encoder and decoder separately as well. The encoder model accepts images and encodes it into a 32-dimensional vector. The decoder decodes the input image. The encoder and decoder are separately developed to test the performance of the autoencoder, as you will see later.

Script 5:

```
1.    encoder = Model(input_layer, encoder_layer1)
2.    encoded_input = Input(shape=(encoding_dim,))
3.    decoder_layer = autoencoder.layers[-1]
4.    decoder = Model(encoded_input, decoder_layer(encoded_
      input))
```

The following script compiles our autoencoder model.

Script 6:

```
1.    autoencoder.compile(optimizer='adadelta', loss='binary_
      crossentropy')
```

And the following script trains the autoencoder model. You can see that the process of compilation of autoencoders in Keras is similar to any other neural network. The model trains for 60 epochs with a batch size of 256. You can see that both the input and output to the **fit()** method for training is the training images. Similarly, for validation, both input and outputs contain the test images. This is because autoencoders are unsupervised and do not require training labels for training.

Script 7:

```
1.   epochs = 60
2.   batch_size = 256
3.
4.   autoencoder.fit(train_images, train_images,
5.                   epochs=epochs,
6.                   batch_size=batch_size,
7.                   shuffle=True,
8.                   validation_data=(test_images, test_
     images))
```

The output from the last five training epochs is as follows.

Output:

```
60000/60000 [==============================] - 2s 37us/step -
loss: 0.1024 - val_loss: 0.1007
Epoch 57/60
60000/60000 [==============================] - 2s 38us/step -
loss: 0.1022 - val_loss: 0.1004
Epoch 58/60
60000/60000 [==============================] - 2s 37us/step -
loss: 0.1020 - val_loss: 0.1002
Epoch 59/60
60000/60000 [==============================] - 2s 38us/step -
loss: 0.1017 - val_loss: 0.1000
Epoch 60/60
60000/60000 [==============================] - 2s 38us/step -
loss: 0.1015 - val_loss: 0.0998
<keras.callbacks.callbacks.History at 0x7f2d631480f0>
```

Our model is trained now. Let's use the encoder and decoder that we created earlier to test the model. Remember, when you train the autoencoder, the encoding and decoding layers that the encoder and decoder use are also trained. Hence, encoders and decoders are capable of encoding and decoding images.

Script 8:

```
1.  encoded_imgs = encoder.predict(test_images)
2.  decoded_imgs = decoder.predict(encoded_imgs)
```

If you check the shape of the encoded_imgs variable, you will see that it contains 10,000 records with 32 dimensions per record, which means that encoder has successfully compressed test images from 784 dimensions to 32 dimensions via the **predict()** method. Next, we call the **predict()** method on the decoder and pass it the encoded/compressed images. The decoder reconstructs a 784-dimensional vector for each compressed image.

Let's print the first five original images in the test set and then the corresponding reconstructed images to see how well our autoencoder is performing.

Script 9:

```
1.  import matplotlib.pyplot as plt
2.
3.  n = 5  # how many digits we will display
4.  plt.figure(figsize=(20, 4))
5.  for i in range(n):
6.      # original images
7.      ax = plt.subplot(2, n, i + 1)
8.      plt.imshow(test_images[i].reshape(28, 28))
9.      plt.gray()
10.     ax.get_xaxis().set_visible(False)
11.     ax.get_yaxis().set_visible(False)
12.
```

```
13.     # reconstructed images
14.     ax = plt.subplot(2, n, i + 1 + n)
15.     plt.imshow(decoded_imgs[i].reshape(28, 28))
16.     plt.gray()
17.     ax.get_xaxis().set_visible(False)
18.     ax.get_yaxis().set_visible(False)
19. plt.show()
```

Output:

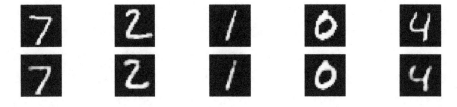

From the output, it is noticeable that the decoder has been successfully able to reconstruct the 784-dimensional images from 32-dimensional compressed image representations. Some loss has occurred in the reconstructed images, as you can see at the top of digit 1 and in digit 4, but overall, the images have been reconstructed quite perfectly. This is how autoencoders are used for image compression and reconstruction. In the next section, you will scrutinize how autoencoders can be used for anomaly detection.

8.3. Autoencoders for Anomaly Detection

Anomaly in a dataset can be defined as deviation from normal behavior exhibited by a majority of the records in a dataset. Autoencoders can be used for clustering, which means that they can also be used for detecting anomalies since clustering records with common behavior are grouped together. Since anomalies exhibit different behaviors than most of the other records, they will be grouped together.

It is important to mention that autoencoders do not label the clusters, i.e., they cannot tell you which records are anomalies. Autoencoders simply divide the data into clusters. It is for you to decide which cluster represents anomalies and which cluster contains normal records.

In this section, you will develop an autoencoder capable of finding anomalies in the banknote records. The autoencoder will be fed with the input features containing information about banknotes that are real, i.e., not fake. The autoencoder will return you a threshold value that can be used to find the anomalous records.

Since in the training set, the anomalous records among the records of real banknotes will be similar to the banknotes that are fake, the threshold can then be used to make a decision about which banknotes are fake, and which are real in the test set.

Let's see how this works with the help of a simple example.

As always, the first step is to import the required libraries.

Script 10:

```
1.   import numpy as np
2.   import matplotlib.pyplot as plt
3.   import pandas as pd
```

The following script imports the banknote dataset. The dataset is also available in the Datasets folder that accompanies this book.

Script 11:

```
1.  banknote_data = pd.read_csv("https://raw.
    githubusercontent.com/AbhiRoy96/Banknote-Authentication-
    UCI-Dataset/master/bank_notes.csv")
2.
3.  banknote_data.head()
```

Output:

	variance	skewness	curtosis	entropy	Target
0	3.62160	8.6661	-2.8073	-0.44699	0
1	4.54590	8.1674	-2.4586	-1.46210	0
2	3.86600	-2.6383	1.9242	0.10645	0
3	3.45660	9.5228	-4.0112	-3.59440	0
4	0.32924	-4.4552	4.5718	-0.98880	0

The dataset contains four features: variance, skewness, curtosis, and entropy of banknotes.

Next, we will divide the dataset into the features and labels. Remember, to train the autoencoder, we only need features and not the labels. The labels will be used later to see how well our autoencoder creates clusters.

Script 12:

```
1.  X = banknote_data.drop(['Target'], axis=1)
2.  y = banknote_data[['Target']]
```

Let's see the data distribution between the fake and real notes.

Script 13:

```
1.  banknote_data['Target'].value_counts()
```

Output:

```
0      762
1      610
Name: Target, dtype: int64
```

The output shows that 762 notes are real, whereas 610 notes are fake. Let's divide the data into the training and test sets.

Script 14:

```
1.   from sklearn.model_selection import train_test_split
2.   X_train, X_test, y_train, y_test = train_test_split(X, y,
     test_size = 0.3, random_state = 0)
```

Script 15:

```
1.   print(X_train.shape)
2.   print(X_test.shape)
```

The training set contains 960 records, while the test set contains 412 records since we divide the original data into a 70 percent training set and a 30 percent test set.

Output:

```
(960, 4)
(412, 4)
```

Next, from the test and training sets, we will remove the fake banknotes and will only keep the real banknotes. The real banknotes are those where the Target column contains 0. The autoencoder will detect anomalous records in the dataset having real records. The anomalous records will be different than the real banknotes. Or, in other words, we can say that the anomalous records will be similar to the records for the fake banknotes. Using this information, we will differentiate between the real and fake banknotes in the test set. The following script filters the fake banknotes from the training set.

Script 16:

```
1.  X_train_T = X_train.copy()
2.  X_train_T['Target'] = y_train
3.  X_train_T = X_train_T[X_train_T['Target']==0]
4.  X_train_T = X_train_T.drop('Target', axis=1)
5.  X_train_T = np.asarray(X_train_T).astype(np.float32)
6.
7.  X_test_T = X_test.copy()
8.  X_test_T['Target'] = y_test
9.  X_test_T = X_test_T[X_test_T['Target']==0]
10. X_test_T = X_test_T.drop('Target', axis=1)
11. X_test_T = np.asarray(X_test_T).astype(np.float32)
```

Next, we import the libraries required to create autoencoders with Keras.

Script 17:

```
1.  import pandas as pd
2.  import numpy as np
3.  import re
4.
5.  from numpy import array
6.  from tensorflow.keras.preprocessing.text import one_hot
7.
8.  from tensorflow.keras.models import Sequential
9.  from tensorflow.keras.layers import Activation, LSTM,
    Dropout, Dense, Flatten, Input, Embedding, Conv1D, Input
10. from tensorflow.keras.models import Model
11. from sklearn.model_selection import train_test_split
12. from tensorflow.keras import regularizers
13. from sklearn.metrics import recall_score, classification_
    report, auc, roc_curve, accuracy_score
```

The following script creates the neural network model for our autoencoder. We have one encoding and one decoding layer. The encoding layer encodes the 4-dimensional input features to two dimensions, and the decoding layer decodes the 2-dimensional compressed features back to four dimensions.

Script 18:

```
1.   epochs = 400
2.   batch_size = 8
3.   input_dim = X_train_T.shape[1]
4.   encoding_dim = 2
5.
6.
7.   input_layer = Input(shape=(input_dim, ))
8.   ## Encoder Layers
9.   encoder_layer1 = Dense(encoding_dim, activation="relu")
     (input_layer)
10.
11.  decoder_output = Dense(input_dim, activation="linear")
     (encoder_layer1)
12.
13.  autoencoder = Model(inputs=input_layer, outputs=decoder_
     output)
14.  autoencoder.summary()
```

Output:

```
Model: "model"
_____
Layer (type)                 Output Shape              Param #
=================================================================
input_1 (InputLayer)         [(None, 4)]               0
_____
dense (Dense)                (None, 2)                 10
_____
dense_1 (Dense)              (None, 4)                 12
=================================================================
Total params: 22
Trainable params: 22
Non-trainable params: 0
_____
```

The following script compiles and then trains the model.

Script 19:

```
1.   autoencoder.compile(metrics=['accuracy'],
2.                        loss='mean_squared_error',
3.                        optimizer='adam')
4.
5.   history = autoencoder.fit(X_train_T, X_train_T,
6.                        epochs=epochs,
7.                        batch_size=batch_size,
8.                        shuffle=True,
9.                        validation_data=(X_test_T, X_test_T),
10.                       verbose=1)
```

The output from the last five epochs is shown below.

Output:

```
Epoch 396/400
67/67 [==========================] - 0s 2ms/step - loss: 0.6606
- accuracy: 0.9660 - val_loss: 0.7477 - val_accuracy: 0.9871
Epoch 397/400
67/67 [==========================] - 0s 2ms/step - loss: 0.6607
- accuracy: 0.9660 - val_loss: 0.7467 - val_accuracy: 0.9871
Epoch 398/400
67/67 [==========================] - 0s 2ms/step - loss: 0.6601
- accuracy: 0.9660 - val_loss: 0.7477 - val_accuracy: 0.9871
Epoch 399/400
67/67 [==========================] - 0s 2ms/step - loss: 0.6606
- accuracy: 0.9660 - val_loss: 0.7471 - val_accuracy: 0.9871
Epoch 400/400
67/67 [==========================] - 0s 2ms/step - loss: 0.6612
- accuracy: 0.9660 - val_loss: 0.7506 - val_accuracy: 0.9871
```

Next, we want to make predictions on the test set. We can use the **predict()** method and pass it our test set.

Script 20:

```
1.   X_test_pred = autoencoder.predict(X_test)
```

The X_test_pred variable contains the autoencoder predicted 4-dimensional representation of the test records. The next step is to find the mean squared error between the values in the actual test records and the predicted test records. Mean squared error will be less for those predicted records that have features values similar to the test records.

Script 21:

```
1.   mean_seq_error = np.mean(np.power(X_test - X_test_pred,
     2), axis=1)
```

Next, to find the records with anomalies, we need to find the threshold value for the means squared error. We will then say that if the mean squared error of a particular predicted record is greater than the threshold, that record is an anomaly, or in other words, the record belongs to a fake banknote, rather than a real note. We can use the ROC curve to find the threshold mean squared error value. The ROC curve returns the threshold value for the mean squared error, which can then be used to detect anomalies. For more details on the ROC curve, see this link.

https://towardsdatascience.com/understanding-auc-roc-curve-68b2303cc9c5

Script 22:

```
1.   false_positive_rate, true_positive_rate, thresholds =
     roc_curve(y_test, mean_seq_error)
2.   print('thresholds', np.mean(thresholds))
3.   auc(false_positive_rate,  true_positive_rate)
```

The output shows that the records with the mean squared error value greater than 2.73 are considered anomalous and can belong to a fake record. The ROC value of 0.97 is very good since the ROC value of 1 is perfect prediction.

Output:

```
thresholds 2.731671437730215
0.9741139846743295
```

Next, we can find the accuracy of the autoencoder for clustering real and fake notes in the test set. In the test set, the records that have predicted mean squared error greater than the threshold are assigned a value of 1, i.e., fake. Else, the record is assigned a value of 0. Next, you can use the **accuracy_score** class from the **sklearn.metrics** module to find the accuracy of the predicted real and fake notes.

Script 23:

```
1.   final_threshold =  np.mean(thresholds)
2.   predicted_Values = [1 if i > final_threshold else 0 for i
     in mean_seq_error]
3.   accuracy_score(y_test,predicted_Values  )
```

Output:

```
0.9150485436893204
```

The output shows an impressive accuracy of 91.50, which shows that our autoencoder is highly successful in clustering real and fake banknotes.

Exercise 8.1

Question 1:

In an autoencoder, the number of nodes in the input layer is
_____ the number of nodes in the output payer:

1. Smaller than

2. Greater than

3. Smaller than or equal to

4. None of the above

Question 2:

An autoencoder is a type of:

1. Reinforcement learning algorithm

2. Supervised learning algorithm

3. Unsupervised learning algorithm

4. Semi-supervised learning algorithm

Question 3:

Among the following, which one is an application of
autoencoders?

1. Image denoising

2. Recommendation System

3. Dimensionality reduction

4. All of the above

Exercise 8.2

Using breast cancer dataset as follows, perform anomaly detection on the patients who have breast cancer. Divide the data into training and test sets. Learn the threshold for detecting anomaly on the training and use the threshold to make predictions on the complete test set. The dataset can be downloaded with the following script:

```
1.   import pandas as pd
2.   from sklearn.datasets import load_breast_cancer
3.   cancer = load_breast_cancer()
4.
5.   bc_data = pd.DataFrame(cancer.data, columns=cancer.
     feature_names)
6.   bc_data['Target'] = pd.Series(cancer.target)
```

From the Same Publisher

Python Machine Learning
https://bit.ly/3gcb2iG

Python Deep Learning
https://bit.ly/3gci9Ys

Python Data Visualization
https://bit.ly/3wXqDJI

Python for Data Analysis
https://bit.ly/3wPYEM2

Python Data
Preprocessing
https://bit.ly/3fLV3ci

Python
for NLP
https://bit.ly/3chlTqm

10 ML Projects Explained
from Scratch
https://bit.ly/34KFsDk

Python Scikit-Learn
for Beginners
https://bit.ly/3fPbtRf

Data Science
with Python
https://bit.ly/3wVQ5iN

Statistics
with Python
https://bit.ly/3z27KHt

Exercise Solutions

Exercise 1.1

Question 1

Which iteration should be used when you want to repeatedly execute a code a specific number of times?

1. For Loop
2. While Loop
3. Both A and B
4. None of the above

   Answer: 1

Question 2

What is the maximum number of values that a function can return in Python?

1. Single Value
2. Double Value
3. More than two values
4. None

   Answer: 3

Question 3

Which of the following membership operators are supported by Python?

1. In
2. Out
3. Not In
4. Both A and C

    Answer: 4

Exercise 1.2

Print the table of integer for 9 using a while loop.

Solution

```
j=1
while j< 11:
    print("9 x "+str(j)+ " = "+ str(9*j))
    j=j+1
```

Output:

```
9 x 1 = 9
9 x 2 = 18
9 x 3 = 27
9 x 4 = 36
9 x 5 = 45
9 x 6 = 54
9 x 7 = 63
9 x 8 = 72
9 x 9 = 81
9 x 10 = 90
```

Exercise 2.1

Question 1

Which function is used at the last step to find the total error in case of logistic regression:

1. Mean Absolute Error
2. Sigmoid Function
3. Mean Squared Error
4. None of the above

   Answer: 2

Question 2

The number of weights + bias should be:

1. Equal to the number of input feature in the data
2. More than the number of input features
3. Less than the number of input features
4. One more than the number of input features

   Answer: 4

Question 3

The purpose of gradient descent is to:

1. Minimize weights
2. Minimize bias
3. Maximize cost
4. Minimize cost

   Answer: 4

Exercise 2.2

Using the following dataset, apply logistic regression function to classify diabetic and non-diabetic patients. Print the accuracy as well. You can take help from section 2.2. in chapter 2.

```
1.  import pandas as pd
2.  import numpy as np
3.
4.  dataset = pd.read_csv("https://raw.githubusercontent.
    com/npradaschnor/Pima-Indians-Diabetes-Dataset/master/
    diabetes.csv")
5.  dataset.head()
```

Solution:

```
1.  X = dataset.drop(['Outcome'], axis=1).values
2.
3.  y = dataset['Outcome'].values
4.
5.  y = y.reshape(y.shape[0],1)
6.
7.  def define_parameters(n_weights):
8.      w = np.random.randn( n_weights, 1)
9.      b = np.random.randn()
10.
11.     return w, b
12.
13. def sigmoid(x):
14.     return 1/(1+np.exp(-x))
15.
16. def sigmoid_der(x):
17.     return sigmoid(x)*(1-sigmoid(x))
18.
19. def predictions(w, b, X):
20.     XW = np.dot(X,w) + b
21.     z = sigmoid(XW)
22.     return z
23.
```

```
24. def find_cost(z,y):
25.     m = y.shape[0]
26.     total_cost = (1/m) * np.sum(np.square(z - y))
27.     return total_cost
28.
29. def find_derivatives(X,y,z):
30.     m = y.shape[0]
31.     dcost_dpred = (1/m)*(z-y)
32.     dpred_dz = sigmoid_der(z)
33.     z_delta = dcost_dpred * dpred_dz
34.     dz_dw = X.T
35.     dw = np.dot( dz_dw , z_delta)
36.     db = np.sum(z_delta)
37.
38.     return dw, db
39.
40.
41. def update_weights(w,b,dw,db,lr):
42.     w = w - lr * dw
43.     b = b - lr * db
44.
45.     return w, b
46.
47. def multi_linear_regression(X, y, lr, epochs):
48.     error_list = []
49.     lenw = X.shape[1]
50.     w,b = define_parameters(lenw)
51.     for i in range(epochs):
52.         z = predictions(w, b, X)
53.         cost = find_cost(z, y)
54.         error_list.append(cost)
55.         dw, db = find_derivatives (X,y,z)
56.         w, b = update_weights(w, b, dw, db,  lr )
57.         if i % 50 == 0 :
58.             print(cost)
59.
60.
61.     return w, b, error_list
62.
```

```
63.
64. lr = 0.05
65. epochs = 1000
66. w, b, error_list = multi_linear_regression(X,y,lr,epochs)
67.
68. z = predictions(w, b, X)
69.
70. y_pred = []
71. for i in z:
72.     if i > 5.0:
73.         y_pred.append(1)
74.     else:
75.         y_pred.append(0)
76.
77. y_true = sum(y.tolist() , [])
78.
79. correct = 0
80. for i in y_true :
81.     if y[i] == y_pred[i]:
82.         correct = correct + 1
83.
84. print("Accuracy: " + str(correct/len(y_true) * 100))
```

Exercise 3.1

Question 1:

In a neural network with three input features, one hidden layer of five nodes, and an output layer with three possible values, what will be the dimensions of weight that connects the input to the hidden layer? Remember, the dimensions of the input data are (m,3), where m is the number of records.

1. [5,3]
2. [3,5]
3. [4,5]
4. [5,4]

   Answer: 2

Question 2:

Which activation function do you use in the output layer in case of multiclass classification problems:

1. Sigmoid
2. Negative log likelihood
3. Relu
4. Softmax

   Answer: 4

Question 3:

Neural networks with hidden layers are capable of finding:

1. Linear Boundaries

2. Non-linear Boundaries

3. All of the above

4. None of the Above

    Answer: 3

Exercise 3.2

Try to classify the following dataset with three classes by implementing a multiclass classification neural network from scratch in Python.

```
1.  import numpy as np
2.  import matplotlib.pyplot as plt
3.
4.  np.random.seed(42)
5.
6.  cat1 = np.random.randn(800, 2) + np.array([0, -2])
7.  cat2 = np.random.randn(800, 2) + np.array([2, 2])
8.  cat3 = np.random.randn(800, 2) + np.array([-3, -3])
9.
10. X = np.vstack([cat1, cat2, cat3])
11.
12. labels = np.array([0]*800 + [1]*800 + [2]*800)
13.
14. y = np.zeros((2400, 3))
15.
16. for i in range(2400):
17.     y[i, labels[i]] = 1
18.
19. x1 = X[:,0]
20. x2 = X[:,1]
```

```
21.
22. plt.figure(figsize=(10,7))
23. plt.scatter(x1, x2, c= y, cmap=plt.cm.coolwarm)
```

`<matplotlib.collections.PathCollection at 0x7f288732e6d8>`

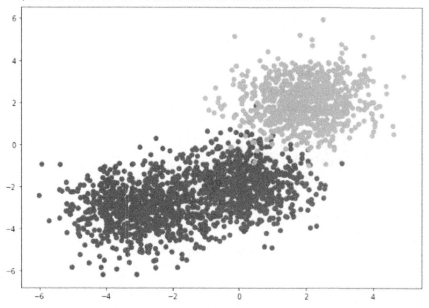

Solution:

```
1.  def define_parameters(weights):
2.      weight_list = []
3.      bias_list = []
4.      for i in range(len(weights) - 1):
5.
6.          w = np.random.randn(weights[i], weights[i+1])
7.          b = np.random.randn()
8.
9.          weight_list.append(w)
10.         bias_list.append(b)
11.
12.     return weight_list, bias_list
13.
14. def softmax(X):
15.     expX = np.exp(X)
```

```
16.        return expX / expX.sum(axis=1, keepdims=True)
17.
18. def sigmoid(x):
19.        return 1/(1+np.exp(-x))
20.
21. def sigmoid_der(x):
22.        return sigmoid(x)*(1-sigmoid(x))
23.
24. def predictions(w, b, X):
25.        zh = np.dot(X,w[0]) + b[0]
26.        ah = sigmoid(zh)
27.
28.        zo = np.dot(ah, w[1]) + b[1]
29.        ao = softmax(zo)
30.        return ao
31.
32. def find_cost(ao,y):
33.
34.        total_cost = np.sum(-y * np.log(ao))
35.        return total_cost
36.
37. def find_derivatives(w, b, X):
38.
39.        zh = np.dot(X,w[0]) + b[0]
40.        ah = sigmoid(zh)
41.
42.        zo = np.dot(ah, w[1]) + b[1]
43.        ao = softmax(zo)
44.
45.        # Backpropagation phase 1
46.
47.        dcost_dzo = (ao-y)
48.        dzo_dwo = ah.T
49.
50.        dwo =  np.dot(dzo_dwo,  dcost_dzo)
51.        dbo = np.sum(dcost_dzo)
52.
53.        # Backpropagation phase 2
54.
```

```
55.      # dcost_wh = dcost_dah * dah_dzh * dzh_dwh
56.      # dcost_dah = dcost_dzo * dzo_dah
57.
58.
59.      dzo_dah = w[1].T
60.
61.      dcost_dah = np.dot(dcost_dzo , dzo_dah)
62.
63.      dah_dzh = sigmoid_der(zh)
64.      dzh_dwh = X.T
65.      dwh = np.dot(dzh_dwh, dah_dzh * dcost_dah)
66.      dbh = np.sum(dah_dzh * dcost_dah)
67.
68.      return dwh, dbh, dwo, dbo
69.
70. def update_weights(w,b,dwh, dbh, dwo, dbo, lr):
71.      w[0] = w[0] - lr * dwh
72.      w[1] = w[1] - lr * dwo
73.
74.      b[0] = b[0] - lr * dbh
75.      b[1] = b[1] - lr * dbo
76.
77.      return w, b
78.
79. def my_multiout_neural_network(X, y, lr, epochs):
80.      error_list = []
81.      input_len = X.shape[1]
82.      output_len = y.shape[1]
83.      w,b = define_parameters([input_len, 10, output_len])
84.
85.      for i in range(epochs):
86.          ao = predictions(w, b, X)
87.          cost = find_cost(ao, y)
88.          error_list.append(cost)
89.          dwh, dbh, dwo, dbo = find_derivatives (w, b, X)
90.          w, b = update_weights(w, b, dwh, dbh, dwo, dbo,
     lr )
91.          if i % 50 == 0 :
92.              print(cost)
```

```
93.
94.       return w, b, error_list
95.
96.  lr = 0.005
97.  epochs = 1000
98.  w, b, error_list = my_multiout_neural_
     network(X,y,lr,epochs)
```

Exercise 4.1

Question 1:

Which of the following loss functions can be used for regression problems:

1. Binary Cross-Entropy
2. Categorical Cross-Entropy
3. Log Likelihood
4. None of the Above

   Answer (4)

Question 2:

We say that a model is overfitting when:

1. Results on the test set are better than the result on the training set
2. Results on both the test and training sets are similar
3. Results on the training set are better than the results on the test set
4. None of the above

   Answer (3)

Question 3:

The number of neurons in the output layer depends upon:

1. The type of problem
2. The number of possible outputs
3. The activation functions
4. The loss functions

Answer (2)

Exercise 4.2

```
1.  import seaborn as sns
2.  import pandas as pd
3.  import numpy as np
4.
5.  from tensorflow.keras.layers import Dense, Dropout,
    Activation
6.  from tensorflow.keras.models import Model, Sequential
7.  from tensorflow.keras.optimizers import Adam
8.
9.  diamond_data = sns.load_dataset('diamonds')
10.
11. diamond_data .head()
```

	carat	cut	color	clarity	depth	table	price	x	y	z
0	0.23	Ideal	E	SI2	61.5	55.0	326	3.95	3.98	2.43
1	0.21	Premium	E	SI1	59.8	61.0	326	3.89	3.84	2.31
2	0.23	Good	E	VS1	56.9	65.0	327	4.05	4.07	2.31
3	0.29	Premium	I	VS2	62.4	58.0	334	4.20	4.23	2.63
4	0.31	Good	J	SI2	63.3	58.0	335	4.34	4.35	2.75

From the diamond dataset above, predict the price of diamond using all the other features.

Tip: Use one-hot encoding to convert categorical variables into numerical variables.

Solution:

```
1.  diamond_data.shape
2.  categorical_data = diamond_data.drop(['cut','color',
    'clarity'], axis=1)
3.
4.  cut_1hot = pd.get_dummies(diamond_data.cut).iloc[:,1:]
5.  color_1hot = pd.get_dummies(diamond_data.color).iloc[:,1:]
6.  clarity_1hot = pd.get_dummies(diamond_data.clarity).
    iloc[:,1:]
7.
8.  diamond_data = pd.concat([categorical_data,cut_1hot,
    color_1hot,clarity_1hot], axis=1)
9.
10. X = diamond_data.drop(['price'], axis=1).values
11.
12. y = diamond_data['price'].values
13.
14. from sklearn.model_selection import train_test_split
15.
16. X_train, X_test, y_train, y_test = train_test_split(X, y,
    test_size=0.2, random_state=40)
17.
18. from sklearn.preprocessing import StandardScaler
19.
20. sc = StandardScaler()
21. X_train = sc.fit_transform(X_train)
22. X_test = sc.transform(X_test)
23.
24. def create_model(learning_rate, dropout_rate):
25.
26.     model = Sequential()
27.     model.add(Dense(100, input_dim=X_train.shape[1],
    activation='relu'))
```

```
28.        model.add(Dropout(dropout_rate))
29.        model.add(Dense(50,  activation='relu'))
30.        model.add(Dropout(dropout_rate))
31.        model.add(Dense(25,  activation='relu'))
32.        model.add(Dropout(dropout_rate))
33.        model.add(Dense(1))
34.
35.        adam = Adam(lr=learning_rate)
36.        model.compile(loss='mean_squared_error', optimizer=adam,
    metrics=['mae'])
37.        return model
38.
39.
40.  dropout_rate = 0.1
41.  epochs = 20
42.  batch_size = 4
43.  learn_rate = 0.001
44.
45.  model = create_model(learn_rate, dropout_rate)
46.
47.  model_history = model.fit(X_train, y_train, batch_
     size=batch_size, epochs=epochs, validation_split=0.2,
     verbose=1)
48.
49.  accuracies = model.evaluate(X_test, y_test, verbose=1)
50.
51.  print("Test Score:", accuracies[0])
52.  print("Test MAE:", accuracies[1])
```

Exercise 5.1

Question 1

What should be the input shape of the input image to the convolutional neural network?

1. Width, Height
2. Height, Width
3. Channels, Width, Height
4. Width, Height, Channels

   Answer: (4)

Question 2

The pooling layer is used to pick correct features even if:

1. Image is Inverted
2. Image is distorted
3. Image is compressed
4. All of the above

   Answer: (4)

Question 3

The ReLu activation function is used to introduce:

1. Linearity
2. Non-linearity
3. Quadraticity
4. None of the above

   Answer: (2)

Exercise 5.2

Using the CFAR 10 image dataset, perform image classification to recognize the image . Here is the dataset :

```
1.  cifar_dataset = tf.keras.datasets.cifar10
```

Solution:

```
1.  (training_images, training_labels), (test_images, test_
    labels) = cifar_dataset.load_data()
2.
3.  training_images, test_images = training_images/255.0,
    test_images/255.0
4.
5.  training_labels, test_labels = training_labels.flatten(),
    test_labels.flatten()
6.  print(training_labels.shape)
7.  print(training_images.shape)
8.
9.  output_classes = len(set(training_labels))
10. print("Number of output classes is: ", output_classes)
11.
12. input_layer = Input(shape = training_images[0].shape )
13. conv1 = Conv2D(32, (3,3), strides = 2, activation= 'relu')
    (input_layer)
14.
15. maxpool1 = MaxPool2D(2, 2)(conv1)
16.
17. conv2 = Conv2D(64, (3,3), strides = 2, activation= 'relu')
    (maxpool1)
18.
19. #conv3 = Conv2D(128, (3,3), strides = 2, activation=
    'relu')(conv2)
20.
21. flat1 = Flatten()(conv2)
22.
23. drop1 = Dropout(0.2)(flat1)
24.
25. dense1 = Dense(512, activation = 'relu')(drop1)
```

```
26. drop2  = Dropout(0.2)(dense1)
27.
28. output_layer = Dense(output_classes, activation=
    'softmax')(drop2)
29.
30. model = Model(input_layer, output_layer)
31.
32. model.compile(optimizer = 'adam', loss= 'sparse_
    categorical_crossentropy', metrics =['accuracy'])
33. model_history = model.fit(training_images, training_labels,
    epochs=20, validation_data=(test_images, test_labels),
    verbose=1)
```

Exercise 6.1

Question 1:

The shape of the feature set passed to the LSTM's input layer should be:

1. Number of Records, Features, Time Steps

2. Time Steps, Features, Number of Records

3. Features, Time Steps, Number of Records

4. Number of Records, TimeSteps, Features

    Answer: 4

Question 2:

To connect the encoder with the decoder layer in many to many sequence problems, which layer is used:

1. Time distributed
2. Repeat vector
3. Dense
4. Softmax

   Answer: 2

Question 3:

Image to text description is an example of:

1. One to One Sequence Problems
2. Many to One Sequence Problems
3. Many to Many Sequence Problems
4. One to Many Sequence Problems

   Answer: 4

Exercise 6.2

Using the Facebook training and testing data provided in the dataset, predict the closing stock price of the Facebook company for the next day.

Solution:

```
1.  import pandas as pd
2.  import numpy as np
3.  fb_complete_data = pd.read_csv("/content/fb_train.csv")
4.
5.  fb_training_processed = fb_complete_data[['Close']].values
6.
7.  from sklearn.preprocessing import MinMaxScaler
8.  scaler = MinMaxScaler(feature_range = (0, 1))
9.
10. fb_training_scaled = scaler.fit_transform(fb_training_
    processed)
11.
12. fb_training_features= []
13. fb_training_labels = []
14. for i in range(60, len(fb_training_scaled)):
15.     fb_training_features.append(fb_training_scaled[i-60:i,
    0])
16.     fb_training_labels.append(fb_training_scaled[i, 0])
17.
18. X_train = np.array(fb_training_features)
19. y_train = np.array(fb_training_labels)
20.
21. X_train = np.reshape(X_train, (X_train.shape[0], X_train.
    shape[1], 1))
22.
23. import numpy as np
24. import matplotlib.pyplot as plt
25. from tensorflow.keras.layers import Input, Activation,
    Dense, Flatten, Dropout,  Flatten, LSTM
26. from tensorflow.keras.models import Model
27.
28.
29.
30. input_layer = Input(shape = (X_train.shape[1], 1))
31. lstm1 = LSTM(100, activation='relu', return_
    sequences=True)(input_layer)
32. do1 = Dropout(0.2)(lstm1)
```

```
33. lstm2 = LSTM(100, activation='relu', return_
    sequences=True)(do1)
34. do2 = Dropout(0.2)(lstm2)
35. lstm3 = LSTM(100, activation='relu', return_
    sequences=True)(do2)
36. do3 = Dropout(0.2)(lstm3)
37. lstm4 = LSTM(100, activation='relu')(do3)
38. do4 = Dropout(0.2)(lstm4)
39.
40. output_layer = Dense(1)(do4)
41. model = Model(input_layer, output_layer)
42. model.compile(optimizer='adam', loss='mse')
43.
44. print(X_train.shape)
45. print(y_train.shape)
46. y_train= y_train.reshape(-1,1)
47. print(y_train.shape)
48.
49. model_history = model.fit(X_train, y_train, epochs=100,
    verbose=1, batch_size = 32)
50.
51.
52.
53. fb_testing_complete_data = pd.read_csv("/content/fb_test.
    csv")
54. fb_testing_processed = fb_testing_complete_
    data[['Close']].values
55.
56. fb_all_data = pd.concat((fb_complete_data['Close'], fb_
    testing_complete_data['Close']), axis=0)
57.
58. test_inputs = fb_all_data [len(fb_all_data ) - len(fb_
    testing_complete_data) - 60:].values
59. print(test_inputs.shape)
60.
61. test_inputs = test_inputs.reshape(-1,1)
62. test_inputs = scaler.transform(test_inputs)
63. print(test_inputs.shape)
64.
```

```
65. fb_test_features = []
66. for i in range(60, 80):
67.     fb_test_features.append(test_inputs[i-60:i, 0])
68.
69. X_test = np.array(fb_test_features)
70. print(X_test.shape)
71.
72. X_test = np.reshape(X_test, (X_test.shape[0], X_test.
    shape[1], 1))
73. print(X_test.shape)
74.
75. y_pred =  model.predict(X_test)
76. y_pred = scaler.inverse_transform(y_pred)
77.
78.
79.
80. plt.figure(figsize=(8,6))
81. plt.plot(fb_testing_processed, color='red', label='Actual
    Facenook Stock Price')
82. plt.plot(y_pred , color='green', label='Predicted Face
    Stock Price')
83. plt.title('Facebook Stock Prices')
84. plt.xlabel('Date')
85. plt.ylabel('Stock Price')
86. plt.legend()
87. plt.show()
```

Exercise 7.1

Question 1

Which of the following is not pre-trained word embeddings?

1. Glove
2. Stanford
3. Peeking
4. All of the above

   Answer: 3

Question 2

What should be the first argument to the Keras Embedding Layer?

1. The input vector dimensions
2. The output vector dimensions
3. The word embedding size
4. The vocabulary size

   Answer: 4

Question 3

Which layer will you need to use if you want to directly connect the Embedding Layer with a Dense Layer?

1. LSTM layer with return_sequence set to False
2. CNN layer with max pooling
3. Flatten layer
4. None of the Above

   Answer: 3

Exercise 7.2

Using the IMDB dataset that we used for sentiment classification in section 7.4, perform sentiment classification using an RNN.

See if you can get better results with RNN as compared to the results in section 7.4.

Solution:

```
1.   import pandas as pd
2.   import numpy as np
3.   import re
4.   import nltk
5.   from nltk.corpus import stopwords
6.
7.   from numpy import array
8.   from tensorflow.keras.preprocessing.text import one_hot
9.   from tensorflow.keras.preprocessing.sequence import pad_
     sequences
10.  from tensorflow.keras.models import Sequential
11.  from tensorflow.keras.layers import Activation, LSTM,
     Dropout, Dense, Flatten, Input,  Embedding, Conv1D, Input
12.  from tensorflow.keras.models import Model
13.  from sklearn.model_selection import train_test_split
14.  from tensorflow.keras.preprocessing.text import Tokenizer
15.  from google.colab import drive
16.  drive.mount('/gdrive')
17.  imdb_data= pd.read_csv("/gdrive/My Drive/datasets/IMDB
     Dataset.csv")
18.
19.  imdb_data.head()
20.
21.  imdb_data.sentiment.value_counts()
22.  X = imdb_data["review"]
23.
24.  y = pd.get_dummies(imdb_data.sentiment, prefix='sent',
     drop_first=True).values
25.  y.shape
```

```
26. def clean_text(doc):
27.
28.     document = remove_tags(doc)
29.
30.     document = re.sub('[^a-zA-Z]', ' ', document)
31.
32.     document = re.sub(r"\s+[a-zA-Z]\s+", ' ', document)
33.
34.     document = re.sub(r'\s+', ' ', document)
35.
36.     return document
37. TAG_RE = re.compile(r'<[^>]+>')
38.
39. def remove_tags(document):
40.     return TAG_RE.sub('', document)
41. X_sentences = []
42. reviews = list(X)
43. for rev in reviews:
44.     X_sentences.append(clean_text(rev))
45. X_train, X_test, y_train, y_test = train_test_split(X_
    sentences, y, test_size=0.20, random_state=42)
46. tokenizer = Tokenizer(num_words=5000)
47. tokenizer.fit_on_texts(X_train)
48.
49. X_train = tokenizer.texts_to_sequences(X_train)
50. X_test = tokenizer.texts_to_sequences(X_test)
51. vocab_size = len(tokenizer.word_index) + 1
52.
53. maxlen = 100
54.
55. X_train = pad_sequences(X_train, padding='post',
    maxlen=maxlen)
56. X_test = pad_sequences(X_test, padding='post',
    maxlen=maxlen)
57. from numpy import array
58. from numpy import asarray
59. from numpy import zeros
60.
61. embedd_dict= dict()
```

```
62. glove_embeddings = open('/gdrive/My Drive/datasets/
    glove.6B.100d.txt', encoding="utf8")
63.
64. for embeddings in glove_embeddings:
65.     embedding_tokens = embeddings.split()
66.     emb_word = embedding_tokens [0]
67.     emb_vector = asarray(  embedding_tokens[1:],
    dtype='float32')
68.     embedd_dict [emb_word] = emb_vector
69.
70. glove_embeddings.close()
71. embedd_mat= zeros((vocab_size, 100))
72. for word, index in tokenizer.word_index.items():
73.     embedding_vector = embedd_dict.get(word)
74.     if embedding_vector is not None:
75.         embedd_mat[index] = embedding_vector
76. embedd_mat.shape
77.
78. embedding_inputs = Input(shape=(maxlen))
79. embedding_layer = Embedding(vocab_size, 100,
    weights=[embedd_mat], trainable=False)(embedding_inputs )
80. lstm1 = LSTM(128, activation='relu', return_
    sequences=True)(embedding_layer)
81.
82. lstm2 = LSTM(64, activation='relu', )(lstm1)
83.
84. drop1 = Dropout(0.2)(lstm2)
85. dense1 = Dense(512, activation = 'relu')(drop1)
86. drop2  = Dropout(0.2)(dense1)
87. output_layer = Dense(1, activation= 'sigmoid')(drop2)
88.
89. model = Model(embedding_inputs, output_layer )
90. model.compile(optimizer='adam', loss='binary_
    crossentropy', metrics=['accuracy'])
91. from tensorflow.keras.utils import plot_model
92. plot_model(model, to_file='model_plot1.png', show_
    shapes=True, show_layer_names=True)
93. history = model.fit(X_train, y_train, batch_size= 128,
    epochs=10, verbose=1, validation_split=0.2)
```

```
94.
95. score = model.evaluate(X_test, y_test, verbose=1)
96. print(score[0])
97. print(score[1])
```

Exercise 8.1

Question 1:

In an autoencoder, the number of nodes in the input layer is
_____ the number of nodes in the output payer:

1. Smaller than
2. Greater than
3. Smaller than or equal to
4. None of the above

   Answer: 4

Question 2:

An autoencoder is a type of:

1. Reinforcement learning algorithm
2. Supervised learning algorithm
3. Unsupervised learning algorithm
4. Semi-supervised learning algorithm

   Answer: 3

Question 3:

Among the following, which one is an application of autoencoders?

1. Image denoising

2. Recommendation System

3. Dimensionality reduction

4. All of the above

    Answer: 4

Exercise 8.2

Using breast cancer dataset as follows, perform anomaly detection on the patients who have breast cancer. Divide this data into training and test sets. Learn the threshold for detecting anomaly on the training and use the threshold to make predictions on the complete test set. The dataset can be downloaded with the following script:

```
1.  import pandas as pd
2.  from sklearn.datasets import load_breast_cancer
3.  cancer = load_breast_cancer()
4.
5.  bc_data = pd.DataFrame(cancer.data, columns=cancer.
    feature_names)
6.  bc_data['Target'] = pd.Series(cancer.target)
```

Note: The following solution is only a vanilla solution on how to perform the task in Exercise 8.2. You can change the dimensions and neural network layers to get better results.

Solution:

```
1.  import numpy as np
2.  import matplotlib.pyplot as plt
3.  from sklearn.datasets import load_breast_cancer
4.  cancer = load_breast_cancer()
5.  bc_data = pd.DataFrame(cancer.data, columns=cancer.
    feature_names)
6.  bc_data['Target'] = pd.Series(cancer.target)
7.  bc_data.head()
8.  bc_data.shape
9.  bc_data['Target'].value_counts()
10. X =  bc_data.drop(['Target'], axis=1)
11. y = bc_data[['Target']]
12. from sklearn.model_selection import train_test_split
13. X_train, X_test, y_train, y_test = train_test_split(X, y,
    test_size = 0.3, random_state = 0)
14. print(X_train.shape)
15. print(X_test.shape)
16. X_train_T = X_train.copy()
17. X_train_T['Target'] = y_train
18. X_train_T = X_train_T[X_train_T['Target']==0]
19. X_train_T = X_train_T.drop('Target', axis=1)
20. X_train_T = np.asarray(X_train_T).astype(np.float32)
21.
22. X_test_T = X_test.copy()
23. X_test_T['Target'] = y_test
24. X_test_T = X_test_T[X_test_T['Target']==0]
25. X_test_T = X_test_T.drop('Target', axis=1)
26. X_test_T = np.asarray(X_test_T).astype(np.float32)
27. import pandas as pd
28. import numpy as np
29. import re
30.
31.
32. from numpy import array
33. from tensorflow.keras.preprocessing.text import one_hot
34.
35. from tensorflow.keras.models import Sequential
```

```
36. from tensorflow.keras.layers import Activation, LSTM,
    Dropout, Dense, Flatten, Input,  Embedding, Conv1D, Input
37. from tensorflow.keras.models import Model
38. from sklearn.model_selection import train_test_split
39. from tensorflow.keras import regularizers
40. from sklearn.metrics import recall_score, classification_
    report, auc, roc_curve, accuracy_score
41.
42. epochs = 800
43. batch_size = 2
44. input_dim = X_train_T.shape[1]
45. encoding_dim = 16
46. hidden_layers_nodes = 8
47.
48. learning_rate = 1e-3
49.
50.
51. input_layer = Input(shape=(input_dim, ))
52. ## Encoder Layers
53. encoder_layer1 = Dense(encoding_dim, activation="relu")
    (input_layer)
54. encoder_layer2 = Dense(hidden_layers_nodes,
    activation="relu")(encoder_layer1)
55.
56. ## Decoder Layers
57. decoder_layer1 = Dense(hidden_layers_nodes,
    activation="relu")(encoder_layer2)
58. decoder_layer2 = Dense(encoding_dim, activation="relu")
    (decoder_layer1)
59. decoder_output = Dense(input_dim, activation="linear")
    (decoder_layer2)
60.
61. autoencoder = Model(inputs=input_layer, outputs=decoder_
    output)
62. autoencoder.summary()
63. autoencoder.compile(metrics=['accuracy'],
64.                     loss='mean_squared_error',
65.                     optimizer='adam')
66.
```

```
67. history = autoencoder.fit(X_train_T, X_train_T,
68.                           epochs=epochs,
69.                           batch_size=batch_size,
70.                           shuffle=True,
71.                           validation_data=(X_test_T, X_test_T),
72.                           verbose=1)
73. X_test_pred = autoencoder.predict(X_test)
74. print(X_test_pred.shape)
75. mean_seq_error = np.mean(np.power(X_test - X_test_pred,
    2), axis=1)
76. mean_seq_error
77. false_positive_rate, true_positive_rate, thresholds =
    roc_curve(y_test, mean_seq_error)
78. print('thresholds', np.mean(thresholds))
79. auc(false_positive_rate, true_positive_rate)
80. final_threshold = np.mean(thresholds)
81. accuracy_score(y_test, [1 if i > final_threshold else 0 for
    i in mean_seq_error])
```